THE
WILD
HORSE

THE
WILD
HORSE

AN ADOPTER'S
MANUAL

BARBARA EUSTIS-CROSS
and NANCY BOWKER

Howell Book House · New York
Maxwell Macmillan Canada · Toronto
Maxwell Macmillan International ·
New York · Oxford · Singapore · Sydney

This book is humbly dedicated to the wild horses and burros

Copyright © 1992 by Barbara Eustis-Cross and Nancy Bowker

Howell Book House
Macmillan Publishing Company
866 Third Avenue
New York, NY 10022

Maxwell Macmillan Canada, Inc.
1200 Eglinton Avenue East
Suite 200
Don Mills, Ontario M3C 3N1

Macmillan Publishing Company is part of the Maxwell Communication Group of Companies.

The illustrations are by Dan Goodwin except for those on pages 91 (James Souder) and 103 through 106 (Nancy Bowker). All photographs are by Nancy Bowker unless otherwise credited.

Certificate of Title on page 203 courtesy of Bureau of Land Management Title page photograph courtesy of Bureau of Land Management, Reno, Nevada

Library of Congress Cataloging-in-Publication Data
Eustis-Cross, Barbara.
    The wild horse : an adopter's manual / Barbara Eustis-Cross and Nancy Bowker.
      p.   cm.
    Includes index.
    ISBN 0-87605-847-0
    1. Wild horse adoption—Handbooks, manuals, etc. 2. Wild horse adoption—United States—Handbooks, manuals, etc. I. Bowker, Nancy. II. Title.
SF360.4.E98 1992
636.1—dc20   91-24040
                                                                  CIP

Macmillan books are available at special discounts for bulk purchases for sales promotions, premiums, fund-raising, or educational use. For details, contact:

Special Sales Director
Macmillan Publishing Company
866 Third Avenue
New York, NY 10022

10 9 8 7 6 5 4 3 2 1
Printed in the United States of America

CONTENTS

FOREWORD

I've always been passionately interested in animals and even though some early hopes of becoming a veterinarian vanished as my acting career flourished, I still make a place for animals in my life.

As President of the William Holden Wildlife Foundation, as a member of other organizations dedicated to protecting endangered species, and as a horsewoman, I can truly appreciate what Barbara Eustis-Cross and Nancy Bowker have done to educate and inform prospective adopters about the wild horse.

No matter how many years' experience we may have with horses, we only know about the domestic horse. The needs of the wild horse are unique in every way. Think for a moment: an animal that has been running free with the herd and foraging in remote places must deal with a totally foreign environment once he is taken from the open range. First he encounters human beings, and then before long a trailer, a barn, a closed-in pasture, the ministrations of vet and farrier. . . .Unless the wild horse can be introduced to his new surroundings gradually and patiently by a knowledgeable owner, the adoption will not be successful.

This excellent book goes a long way toward helping owners make the adoption a success and it also assures them that the scruffy-looking creatures they take home from the BLM Adoption Center will in time make the transition (if not transformation!) to fit, healthy horses that can be trained for anything: ranch work, trail riding, jumping and even driving.

Actually, the book does something else also. It reminds us that not all wild and beautiful animals are continents away.

Stefanie Powers

ACKNOWLEDGMENTS

Nancy Bowker thanks everyone (horses included!) who contributed to this book:

Lyn Kamer and Robin Rivello, who, with their great enthusiasm for the value of wild horses, generously shared their time and wide knowledge of horses.

Gene Nunn and Owen Badgett, for their technical assistance and their sage words of cowboy wisdom.

The following horsewomen and men who gave their time, information and/or photos: Loretta Pambianchi, Hedy Strauss, Tom Porter, Iris Fitzpatrick, Loretta McCartney, Debra Wolf, Glenda Williams and Naomi Tyler.

Also: Sharon Kipping, Ron Harding, Don Smurthwaite, Fred Wyatt, Peter Bierbach and Robert Stewart.

My coauthor and friend, Barbara Eustis-Cross, who has worked unceasingly with and for wild horses, helping many a horse to live and breathe another day.

Our editor Madelyn Larsen, for her kind assistance and her belief in this project from the beginning.

On a personal note: my husband Russ, whose support and sense of humor enabled me to work on this; a wonderful artist and father, James Souder; and the memory of my mother, Marianne Souder, a devoted mother and librarian who helped me get my first horse and instilled in me a love of books.

For morale: Carol Vento, Mitzi Bondy, Melinda Souder, Laurie Pfeifer, Judy Lewis, Sylvia Williams and Judy Hyslop.

And finally, my amazing daughter, Jessica, who with the following words, echoes the effect horses have on us all: "We got the whole United States of America . . . Somebody must be out there hugging a horse."

Barbara Eustis-Cross thanks Joe Dendy, D.V.M., Craig London, D.V.M., Thomas Talbot, D.V.M., and Danette Weich, D.V.M., for editing the chapters dealing with diet, illness, and medical subjects. Also my thanks to Dr. William Ryan, director of communications for Fort Dodge Laboratories, for allowing us to use extensive material from their booklet "Managing Your Horse's Health."

Owen Badgett and Gene Nunn, who were born in the saddle and took the time, almost daily, after working all day with wild horses and burros, to read and reread chapters.

Callie Thornburgh and Danny Brown, who have helped me out of more than one "wreck" and believe in my work.

Nancy Bowker, who brought East Coast polish to Western savvy and gained a whole "passel" of admirers.

Brian and Brooke, who understood and gave up new shoes and dinners so we could take just one more sick, injured or orphaned wild horse or burro.

But especially Dan Goodwin, who took time from his commissioned work to do the drawings for the book and took care of the horses and ranch so I could write.

INTRODUCTION

The wild horse movement as we know it today had its beginning in a small country courthouse in Storey County, Nevada, in 1952. Edward ("Tex") Gladding presented a petition signed by 147 citizens protesting an application for a permit to use airplanes to chase down wild horses destined for the slaughteryard. Velma B. Johnston presented photographs from an earlier such roundup that showed wild horses bleeding and half dead, crushed into a truck. The Storey County Board of Commissioners banned the spotting and pursuit of wild horses by planes in their county.

Although advocates for wild horses were not new, Velma Johnston became the focal point for wild horse supporters throughout the United States. Ironically, she would become famous by a name she was given in 1955, when a heckler in the Nevada State Senate Chamber unflatteringly referred to her as "Wild Horse Annie." The name caught on as Wild Horse Annie brought together people from all walks of life to help fight for wild horses and burros.

The fight did not end in Nevada with the 1959 law that prohibited the chasing and capture of wild horses on public lands with ve-

hicles and aircraft. Wild Horse Annie led the struggle to prevent
the inhumane capture practices of wild horses to the United States
Congress. She also wanted assurance that some wild horses would
always be free to roam public lands and that if such horses became
too numerous they would "be mercifully thinned out, not wiped
out."

On December 15, 1971, Congress passed the Wild Free-Roaming
Horse and Burro Act (PL 92-195) to implement laws relating to
wild horses and burros on public lands. The objective of the regulations was to provide criteria and procedures for protecting,
managing, and controling wild horses and burros as a "recognized
component" of the public land environment. This meant that wild
horses and burros now had a legal right to live on public lands.
The horses and burros would share this right with native wildlife
such as deer and privately owned domestic cattle, whose owners
leased the public lands from the Bureau of Land Management
(BLM) and the Forest Service. Horses and burros on Department
of Defense or Park Service lands were not protected by the law.

The law gave responsibility for the management and protection
of these animals to the U.S. Department of the Interior and through
the BLM to the Department of Agriculture through the Forest Service.

With the passage of the law, horses and burros could not be
removed for commercial or private use, and it also confined them
to specific areas. As the populations of confined animals grew,
many horses and burros began to face starvation. Clearly something
had to be done to prevent the death of the excess population.
From 1971 until the BLM took over the adoption program in 1976,
Wild Horse Organized Assistance (WHOA) adopted out approximately 10,000 wild horses. In 1978, with the passage of the Public
Rangelands Improvement Act (PL 95-154), the U.S. government
was permitted to transfer ownership of up to four animals a year
each to individual adopters who had given the animals one year
of humane care and treatment. Horses rounded up on lands not
protected by the law were adopted by hands-on organizations such
as the Life is for Everything Foundation (LIFE) and WHOA.

In 1982 LIFE asked Barbara Eustis-Cross to transfer from their
wildlife rehabilitation program to a temporary project caring for and
finding homes for 78 burros. She had handled everything from

mountain lions to hummingbirds for the previous twelve years, so how hard could it be? She rapidly became aware of the enormity and the complexity of the problem of caring for and training wild burros and horses.

Although younger horses adopted through the BLM Adopt-A-Horse or Burro program readily found homes, too often an animal arrived at a new home and found inadequate fencing and little or no understanding of its special needs. What started out as a desire to save a wild horse often ended in unintended abuse.

In 1984 the LIFE Foundation established a permanent equine center in California that has handled as many as 268 wild horses and burros a year. The equine center has become not just a place "to put" wild horses and burros but also a unique means by which the physical and psychological needs and the behavior of these animals could be understood. In addition to studying the physiology and problems of the wild horse and burro, the center offers hands-on training classes, seminars, and counseling for the new adopter. Many of the techniques developed at the center are now being used throughout the United States and in other countries that have wild horses.

While Barbara was establishing the equine center in California, Nancy Bowker, on the East Coast, was interviewing adopters and publishing many helpful articles about training the wild horse. But both of us felt a need to provide more detailed information to adopters, and so this book was written with you in mind in the hope that the information we share will help you understand the needs of your newly adopted horse. It is not intended to be the only answer to every question. We want it to be the ground floor, the beginning of your learning. With knowledge, self-confidence, and an understanding of your horse, you will learn to find the style and methods that work best for you.

Many books and even videotapes teach how to gentle and train horses. You have the opportunity, therefore, to continue to learn. Just as no two human beings are alike, no two horses are exactly alike. As your horse learns to understand what you want, you will learn to understand what he is telling you.

We read about some adopters who gentle their wild horse successfully and then return to adopt a second horse. What secret do these people have? Perhaps above all they are realists who acknowledge that we can't adopt a horse and ride off into the sunset the next day. Flicka and the Black Stallion are childhood fantasies.

Wild horses, once gentled and taught not to fear us, are more trainable and more loyal and have more heart than most horses around. With their smooth ground-covering gait and strong hooves and legs, they are perfect trail and pleasure horses. Wild horses have been known to put in a hard week on the ranch and be ready on the weekend to be shown in pleasure, driving, jumping and dressage classes. Such versatility affirms that they are living symbols of spirit and courage. May wild horses always grace our public lands and may we be deserving of the privilege to own one!

Despite all odds the wild equines have survived. But wild horses and burros need the help of caring people to survive. Otherwise, their loss will be ours.

.1.

BEFORE YOU ADOPT

ongratulations on your interest in adopting one of America's wild horses! Across the country owners of wild horses are discovering the true value of these intelligent, hard-working and sure-footed animals.

Some people who decide they want to save a wild horse do not intend to use the horse; instead they want to turn him out to pasture to live out his days. Unfortunately, this seldom works to the horse's benefit. Wild horses are herd animals that depend on other members of the band or herd for physical and mental well-being. Without this interaction with his own species or a substitute, such as a human companion, the wild horse becomes a ghost of his true self. Additional problems arise if the wild horse becomes ill or if basic equine husbandry, such as hoof trimming, cannot be done. We sincerely hope that anyone who wishes to adopt a wild horse is looking for a friend and companion and not a yard ornament.

These horses are frightened of new people, places and things. Because of this they will act "wild." Yet the wild horse and the domestic horse are alike in many ways. Both fear the unknown

BLM WRANGLER DRIVES WILD HORSES TOWARD THE CHUTE LEADING TO THE TEMPORARY CORRAL IN THE OWYHEE MOUNTAINS, IDAHO. (BLM PHOTO BY DON SMURTHWAITE)

and will react by trying to run or escape from something that frightens them. In the wild horse this instinct to flee is more highly developed than it is in most domestic horses. You may be able to approach, touch and ride a trained domestic horse immediately, but a wild horse will require time to adjust to everything from feed and housing to trusting human beings. Consequently there will be much to think about before you decide to adopt, special preparations before you bring your horse home and precautions that will prevent injury to yourself and your horse during the gentling process.

Although only one member of the family may be adopting a wild horse, everyone will be affected by the decision. The hours necessary to gentle and train a wild horse may put additional pressures or responsibilities on family members. Even if the horse is not being adopted for family use, make sure the other members of your family are willing to support your decision in adopting a wild horse.

TIMING AND FITNESS

Many factors will determine how long it will take before your wild horse can be ridden. In general, a domestic horse is ready to carry a rider on his back when he is 2 to 2½ years old. Most domestic horses will receive 30 to 60 days training to reach the "green broke" stage. At this stage a horse knows the basic commands, signals and cues and is comfortable with a rider on its back.

Your adopted wild horse will require additional time to recover from the stresses of roundup, the adoption process and settling in to your home or boarding facility. In addition to age, the physical condition and weight of your horse at the time of adoption will have to be considered. It may take as long as six months for your horse to be physically fit before you can begin actual training, but ground work, or the gentling of your wild horse, should start right away.

Many factors contribute to the growth of horses. While a domestic horse gets approximately the same amount of high-protein feed year-round and is protected from winter weather, the growth of wild horses is strongly regulated by the natural environment. During the spring and summer months they grow rapidly, while in the fall and winter seasons they show little or no growth as forage becomes scarce. The wild horse's body utilizes body fat and available feed to produce body heat, not growth, during the cold season. As a result, the wild horse does not achieve true adult size until he is four to seven years old. This natural growth pattern may contribute to the high bone density found in wild horses and account for their strong legs and bone structure. Although you can

THE WILD HORSE'S GROWTH IS DETERMINED BY THE FORAGE AVAILABLE.
(PHOTO COURTESY OF BLM, BILLINGS, MONTANA)

begin getting a wild horse used to a saddle and some weight on his back, it is advisable to wait until the horse is 2½ to 3 years old for the daily workouts of green breaking. Your veterinarian can best advise you when your horse is ready to carry full weight, and for what type of riding, without damaging his back, legs and knees.

Besides physical condition and age, your horse's mental readiness will also determine how long it will take for you to ride him. Some horses will be gentled and green broke in as little as three months, while others may take as long as a year. There is no such thing as an "average" wild horse, so it is impossible to establish a formula for the length of time between adoption and when he can be ridden.

In general, a minimum of an hour a day should be allowed for the care and training of a newly adopted wild horse. If you don't have the time it takes to train a wild horse, it may be better for you to adopt an already trained former wild horse. Many wild horse organizations have lists of gentled and trained wild horses for sale.

TYPES OF WILD HORSES

The type of wild horse you choose will depend largely on how you intend to use your horse. If you plan to use it for farm work, size may be a determining factor. If your horse is headed for the show ring, a balanced conformation and pleasing head will be important. Some wild horses are pacers or naturally gaited, a plus if you're looking for a dressage horse. A pleasure, trail or endurance horse will need strong legs and hooves, a smooth gait and calm disposition. While a short, stocky horse may be suited for trail riding or mountain climbing, it might not be the best choice for jumping or dressage.

Once you have decided how you will use your horse, talk to people who participate in that activity. Ask them what they feel are the necessary requirements of a horse intended for that discipline. It is wise to listen to what others say, but the final decision must be yours. In the end, it is you and your horse who must work together.

How you relate to a particular horse is as important as the conformation, size or breed. A tall, leggy horse you cannot communicate with is far less likely to clear a jump than a shorter horse who is willing. But do not expect your horse to participate in activities that are beyond his physical capabilities.

The size, conformation and type of wild horse you adopt will depend largely on what area of the United States he is captured

THIS TWO-YEAR-OLD MARE FROM THE COSO MOUNTAINS IN CALIFORNIA SHOWS A NATURAL TENDENCY TO PACE.

from. Very few wild horses are Mustangs or even carry Mustang blood. The Mustang is a true breed descended from horses brought to North America by the Spanish. Although a few herds and ranges of Mustang types are scattered throughout the United States, most wild horses are descended from horses that were turned loose on winter pasture by working ranches or that were given to ranchers by the U.S. Cavalry to mix and breed with wild horses to supply the Army with mounts. Later, as the working ranches disappeared or through government takeover of public and private land, horses escaped or were abandoned. These "wild horses" are, in reality, feral (domestic turned wild) horses. Often they or their forebears have been "wild" for less than twenty years.

While one area of the country may produce a predominately stocky, Quarter Horse type, another area may produce horses with the characteristics of the Thoroughbred, Standardbred, draft, Morgan, Arabian, or even the true Mustang type.

The horse you choose will depend greatly on who will use him. A smaller Mustang-type horse may suit a child, but a growing teen-

THE SHAPE OF THIS STALLION'S HEAD SUGGESTS AN ARABIAN BACKGROUND.

APPALOOSAS FROM THE WARM SPRINGS HERD MANAGEMENT AREA, HARNEY COUNTY, OREGON. (COURTESY OF RON HARDING, BLM, BURNS, OREGON)

JOHN WALSH WITH ABIGAIL, AN EXAMPLE OF THE LARGER, DRAFT-TYPE
WILD HORSE. SHE IS FROM THE OWYNEE RANGE IN NEVADA.

TWO-YEAR-OLD FILLIES FROM THE KIGER HERD MANAGEMENT AREA.
THESE MUSTANGS ARE BELIEVED TO CLOSELY RESEMBLE THE ORIGINAL
SPANISH BARB HORSES OF THE CONQUISTADORES. (COURTESY RON HARDING, BLM,
BURNS, OREGON)

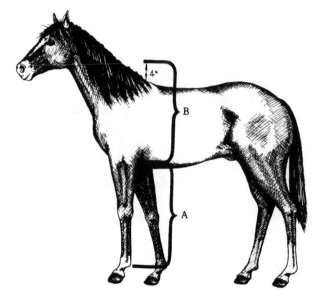

TO ESTIMATE YOUR HORSE'S ADULT HEIGHT, MEASURE THE INCHES FROM
THE FETLOCK TO THE ELBOW (A); THEN MEASURE FROM THE ELBOW TO
THE WITHERS (B). IF A IS LARGER THAN B, WITH GOOD CARE AND FOOD
YOUR HORSE WILL PROBABLY GROW SO THAT B IS AS LARGE AS A.

ager will need one that will still be large enough a few years ahead.
Adults must take into consideration their height and weight in
determining the size of horse that is best for them.

Horses gathered from the Pryor Mountain Range in Montana
average 13.2 hands (54 inches) at the withers, while horses from
the Modock Range in northern California often reach 16 hands (64
inches) or more. The average wild horse is 14.2 hands tall.

The age, geographical area, type of wild horse and even the
condition of his native range affects the final adult size of the horse.
The Bureau of Land Management (BLM) wild horse specialist at
the adoption site or the wild horse organization representative
where you adopt your horse can tell you the likely adult size the
horse you are interested in will attain. With good nutrition and
care some small, underdeveloped two-year-old wild horses have
been known to grow an additional 4 to 8 inches by the age of
seven.

THE AGES OF A HORSE

Wild horses are available at almost every age. The age you choose will depend on your experience with horses, how much time you have to spend in gentling and training and how soon you want to ride your horse.

A weanling is a young horse, usually four to six months old, who has just been taken, or weaned, from its mother. When adopted, it will need additional food supplements, such as Borden's Foal-Lac Pellets, to insure that it has the proper amount of calcium for proper bone growth. A weanling has the best chance for reaching its full potential of height and development because it will have been on a good diet for the longest period of time before adulthood. If you are inexperienced with horses and do not have someone to help you with the training of your adopted horse, the weanling may be a good choice for you. Removed from its mother and other supportive herd members, the weanling becomes lonely very fast and thus will take less time to adjust to human companionship than an older horse. If you choose a weanling, however, you will have to wait several years before you can ride it.

A yearling is a horse twelve months old, although a horse under two is sometimes called a long yearling. At this age the horse's mind is still very flexible and willing to learn. In his natural environment a wild yearling is still dependent on older members of the herd. This dependency will be more rapidly transferred to you than it would with a more cautious older horse. Because yearlings are not fully developed they may be physically easier to handle. If you are unfamiliar with handling a horse and have the time, horses under two years of age seem to develop a special bond with adopters and may be a good choice for you.

Horses two and three years old are usually more mature not only in physical development but also in personality. At this age, most fillies and colts have been run off by the stallion, the fillies to join another band to breed and the colts to join bachelor bands or form a harem of their own. The instinct for flight is more fully developed and the horse will be less willing to accept human companionship. Acceptance will come, but it will come slowly. Once your horse has settled in and has become physically fit, you can begin green breaking at this age.

A limited number of wild horses four to six years old have received some training through one of the BLM Prison Training Programs and are available for adoption. These horses have been handled by inmates from one of the four corrections departments in the country working with wild horses. These institutions are located in California, Colorado, New Mexico and Wyoming. The amount, type and quality of training will depend on the individual handlers within each program. Some of the horses have halter training only, while others are green broke. It will be important to discuss the amount of training the horse has had with the BLM representative at the adoption facility. If it is broken to ride, ask to see the horse ridden. You may have to arrange a time that is convenient for the BLM wranglers. If a horse is halter broken, ask to see him turned loose, caught, haltered and led. If the horse does not respond willingly, select another horse. If you are not able to see the horse worked, select another horse that you can see worked or a horse that has not been handled at all. Do not accept a halter-broken horse that you cannot see handled. Retraining a head-shy horse or one that is improperly trained is much harder than gentling a horse that has not been handled at all.

MALE OR FEMALE?

Whether you choose a male or a female to adopt is really a matter of personal choice, although some consideration should be given to different housing requirements, expenses and the personality traits of the sexes. If you already have horses at home, you may want to adopt a horse of the same sex. Some horse trainers feel there is less competition when mares are placed with mares or geldings are placed with other geldings. This rule does not apply if you have a stallion at home already.

A stallion is a male horse capable of mating with a mare and producing offspring. Most domestic stallions that are used for breeding purposes are trained from a young age and will mount a mare only on a command or signal from the handler. Usually stallions that are used as riding horses are also trained from an early age to ignore mares or other stallions. A wild stallion has not had this training and may be difficult to retrain. Although wild stallions have been known to be gentled and trained into fine riding animals, they are not a good choice for the average adopter. Some BLM facilities, such as those in California, castrate all stallions before adoption and will not adopt out a stallion except by special request.

It would be advisable to check into local zoning and animal-control laws regarding stallions. Most areas restrict the neighborhood and the type of corral a stallion may be kept in. Also some commercial boarding facilities may not accept a stallion or may require an additional fee.

If the horse you choose at the adoption facility is a stallion, you may want to make arrangements with the BLM person in charge to have the animal castrated before you bring it home. If you adopt at a satellite adoption facility, arrangements should be made with your veterinarian to castrate the horse when he is adjusted to his new surroundings, eating well and more easily handled. Your veterinarian can best advise you when your horse is ready. Gelding your stallion will not change his personality, but it will make him more predictable and easier to handle.

A LEGEND IN HIS OWN TIME, MESTENO IS ONE OF THE ORIGINAL KIGER MUSTANG STALLIONS. HE IS MORE THAN TWENTY YEARS OLD AND STILL HAS A BAND OF MARES WITH HIM ON THE RANGE. THE NOTCH IN HIS RIGHT EAR IS FROM FIGHTING ANOTHER STALLION. (COURTESY OF RON HARDING, BLM, BURNS, OREGON)

After a stallion has been castrated he is called a gelding. Some horse handlers believe geldings are more even tempered than stallions or mares. Geldings have a tendency to fight less with other horses.

A filly is a female horse under the age of four that has not been bred, and a mare is a female horse that has been bred or is over the age of four. Although some mares may exhibit signs of nervousness when they are in season, most show little, if any, difference in personality during this time.

ADOPTING A PAIR

If you adopt a mare over the age of two, there is a possibiilty that she may be pregnant. Often wild horses do not exhibit the round, full-belly look usually associated with pregnancy until the last trimester, or they may not show at all. Even if your veterinarian is not able to give your mare a complete pregnancy examination, he or she will be able to teach you what signs to look for.

Adopting a pair, a mother and foal, is both an exciting idea and one that will bring additional responsibilities. A mare with a foal is most likely to be protective of her young and may be less responsive to you because she has her foal to communicate with. Her attention span will be shorter when she is worried about her foal or if her udders become full and uncomfortable. A mare with a foal is usually over three years old and therefore may be more set in her ways. A common problem arises when the pair comes home: the foal responds faster in making friends than the adult wild mare does. Soon the foal becomes the favorite, and the mare gets less and less attention.

The foal will need to be weaned at five to six months of age. To do this you will need a separate corral, preferably out of sight of the mare, so additional expenses must be considered. But if you are willing to do twice the work, you may end up having twice the fun!

OTHER CONSIDERATIONS

Wild horses come in all colors. While coloring may indicate possible breed background, it cannot determine the personality or temperament of a horse. A horse that is all white or that has a large amount of white on his face may require special care. He may develop photosensitivity to the sun on sensitive areas such as the nose and around the eyes. Your veterinarian can best advise you if you feel you have a problem developing or want more information.

Matching your personality to the horse you adopt is important for achieving a happy partnership. Be honest with yourself in deciding what type of horse you need and will enjoy the most. If you are a shy, quiet person, a bold or aggressive horse may be too much for you to handle. Judging a horse's personality by watching it in the corral at the adoption center or holding facility is a challenge, but knowing what you want before you adopt will make the decision easier.

FACE MARKINGS. FROM TOP LEFT: BALD-FACED, STAR, BLAZE, STRIPE, SNIP AND STAR AND STRIPE.

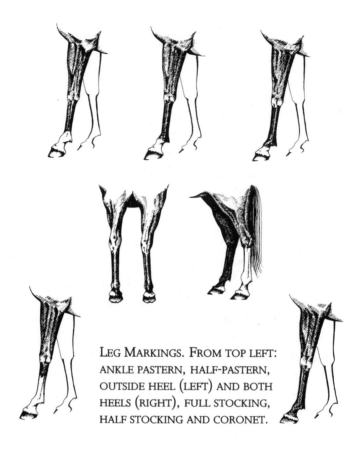

LEG MARKINGS. FROM TOP LEFT:
ANKLE PASTERN, HALF-PASTERN,
OUTSIDE HEEL (LEFT) AND BOTH
HEELS (RIGHT), FULL STOCKING,
HALF STOCKING AND CORONET.

Let's look again at some of the things you should consider before you adopt a wild horse:

- Do you have the time?
- What will you use your adopted horse for?
- Do you want to ride your horse right away?
- What size horse do you need?
- How old a horse do you want?
- Which sex is best for you?
- What type of personality best suits you?
- Who will feed the horse if you are not available?

Once you have thought about these questions and any others that may come up in discussing your desire to adopt a wild horse with your family, you will know whether adopting is for you.

If the answer is yes or maybe, then send for the booklet "So You'd Like to Adopt a Wild Horse or Burro?" from your closest BLM Adopt-A-Horse office (see pages 201 to 204). This pamphlet contains general information about adopting and brief answers to common questions. It will also include an application form.

It is important to find out how the BLM district in your area handles adoption applications. Some districts preapprove applications by mail; others do not. Call or write beforehand so you won't be disappointed when you arrive at the adoption center.

Owning a horse is not inexpensive, and it is important that you have a realistic idea of the costs involved before you purchase a horse. Look at some of the expenses you will have and estimate what it will cost to care for your horse properly:

One-Time Costs

Housing at home
  Pipe corral or
  Wood corral
  Water container
  Feeder
  Shelter

Equipment
  Halter
  Cotton rope (approximately 20'–25' long)
  Buggy or longe whip
  Assorted brushes and combs
  Leather gloves

Other Health Expenses
  Veterinarian (First Exam)
  Castration for stallion
  First-Aid kit

Expenses at adoption
  Adoption Fee
  Transport from Adoption

Continual Costs

Housing at a boarding facility
   Monthly charge
   Additional charges for salt, supplemental feed, etc.

Feed at home
   Hay
   Mineral salt block
   Vitamins/supplemental feeds

Other Health Expenses
   Twice yearly physical
   Vaccinations/worming
   Fly control

After gentling continuing expense
   Farrier (every 8 weeks)
   Professional training (optional)

If, after examining the financial obligations and responsibilities of caring for a wild horse and the training that will be necessary before you have a gentle riding horse, you still dream of owning a wild horse, you are about to participate in one of the most wonderful experiences of your life.

.2.

HOUSING

Where you will stable your horse will depend on many factors, including how much room you have, local zoning regulations and animal control laws.

It is preferable, when possible, to stable your newly adopted wild horse at home. Keeping your horse at home allows you to go out to the corral several times during the day just to say hello. The more exposure your new horse has to you during the early days, the more quickly he will realize that you are not a threat and the sooner friendship can be etablished.

CORRALS AND STABLES

If you are thinking about stabling your horse at home, there are a number of factors to consider. The type of material, the size and even the placement of the enclosure you choose can not only protect your horse but also ease the basic care requirements and training to come later. All too often new adopters find themselves with a runaway horse that has gone through, over or under an inadequate fence. Or worse, they have a horse that becomes injured during an attempt to escape.

The corral must be situated where a horse trailer can back up even with the gate, without gaps, when your horse is delivered. If your horse trailer has a gate that opens to the side, you must securely block off the opposite side when the trailer is in position to unload the horse. A space of up to 3 feet can be blocked with plywood. For a larger gap, you will have to construct an unloading chute.

The corral gate should be wide enough to allow both you and your horse to walk in and out of the corral together, without crowding.

Remember that the first time out of the corral may be as traumatic for your horse as was the first time going in, and you will need room to maneuver safely.

Several types of corrals are used, depending on the age, size and disposition of the horse involved. For a single horse six months or older and in good health, the LIFE Foundation recommends a pipe corral 24'-by-24' (or a minimum total of 400 square feet), at least 6 feet high with five rails and a 6-foot or 8-foot gate. The rails should be heavy-gauge pipe with a diameter of 1⅞".

Some commercial corrals provide a bottom rail that rests on the ground. A horse can paw at this rail and catch a hoof between the rail and the ground, resulting in needless suffering, permanent damage or major veterinary bills that could have been easily prevented. If your corrals have a bottom rail, remove it or bury it to help prevent this type of injury.

Wild horses have been known to crawl under a bottom rail and escape, although this is more common with burros. A resting horse may discover itself half in and half out of a corral if the bottom rail is too high. Bottom rails should be no more than 18 inches from the ground.

The 24'-by-24' size will allow you to begin initial training inside this enclosure as the horse becomes emotionally secure in its new confinement. Any enclosure smaller than this will not allow your horse the "flight space" it needs psychologically. Larger enclosures would allow your horse too much space during adjustment and

WHEN HORSES CHALLENGE THE FENCING, ACCIDENTS CAN HAPPEN. MAKE SURE YOUR ENCLOSURE IS SAFE FOR YOUR HORSE.

later, during training. Additionally, larger corrals will allow your horse enough running room to attempt to jump or crash through the fence. Although it is possible for wild horses to clear a 6-foot fence from a standing position, the average adopter will not be faced with this problem. By placing the highest rail above the horse's eye level, a barrier is created that will deter most horses.

The basic requirements can be met with wood, but even an 800-pound horse hitting this type of fence with its full body weight can break wooden rails. Posts should be placed no more than 8 feet apart with at least 3 feet set into the ground for strength. Rails should be of 2"-by-6" lumber nailed onto the inside of the corral posts for added strength, with no more than 10 inches between them.

One problem with wood is the tendency of livestock to chew on it. Not only is this destructive to the fence, but it can also cause physical damage to the horse. Make sure none of the wood or posts have been treated with chemicals that are poisonous to animals. Coating the fence with a commercial chemical repellent specifically manufactured for use with livestock is recommended.

Although welded wire has been accepted by the BLM, its use is not recommended. Regardless of the quality or the strength of the wire, a panicked or frightened horse is capable of going through it, even with a top rail. The escape or possibility of injury to hooves increases with the use of welded wire.

Although in some circumstances they may be your only choice, box stalls are not recommended. The small space they afford may make it difficult for you to maneuver safely while gentling your horse, and the closed-in feeling may be psychologically difficult

NOTICE HOW EASILY THIS FOAL'S LEGS AND FEET COULD BE CAUGHT IN THIS WELDED WIRE FENCE. (PHOTO BY BARBARA EUSTIS-CROSS)

for the horse to accept. Also because most barn-type box stalls have the opening facing a center aisle, you may be faced with the difficult situation of getting your horse down the aisle into the stall. Box stalls are accepted by the BLM only if they are at least 144 square feet, well drained, well ventilated and cleaned regularly, and if the animal is given daily exercise. Box stalls without access to an adjoining corral for exercise on a daily basis will not qualify as adequate facilities for a newly adopted wild horse.

The BLM requires that horses be provided with shelter. Remember that a wild horse will not naturally seek cover where he is boxed in, thus preventing sight of possible enemies and easy escape routes. Although some wild horses will begin to use a shelter in a short period of time, others may never do so. A run-in shelter, a simple three-sided structure with a roof, should be sufficient in warm-weather climates. Shelter posts should be heavy enough to withstand your horse running into the poles. On the Plains and in Eastern areas, a fully enclosed shelter may be necessary. Check with your local BLM office to find out what the exact requirements are for your area.

A telephone pole or some other heavy restraining post placed midway along one section of the corral will help with training later.

This post should be a minimum of 6 feet above the ground and approximately 12 inches around. At least one-third of the post should be sunk in the ground. A 6-foot post would have 3 feet below the ground. Depending on your soil, you may need to set the pole in concrete. You will also need to permanently fix a sheet of ¾″ plywood behind the post on the inside of the corral. This should be high enough to prevent the horse from getting his legs caught in the corral if he struggles when tied up.

If you do not have a round training pen that is directly attached to your corral, it is a simple matter to make any 24′-by-24′ corral into a round pen by wiring a single sheet of plywood across each corner. Make sure there are no sharp wires pointing into the corral.

FEEDING AND WATERING

Wild horses may not be comfortable with the many types of automatic water units and other containers domestic horses use. A heavy, 32-gallon rubber trash can or a 32-gallon muck bucket (for example, one made by Rubbermaid) is a good choice for temporarily providing water for your horse. If your horse panics and runs into this type of container, little if any damage will occur to horse or receptacle. You can easily remove this type of container when you are training your horse and also easily add medication to the water if your horse becomes ill. Metal trash containers have a tendency to bend and break, leaving sharp edges that can cut and injure the horse, so they are not acceptable. Later, a more permanent water system can be used.

Because the horse's natural eating position is head down, the preferred feeder is one that allows the horse to eat in this position. The same type of 32-gallon muck bucket used for a temporary water system can be used for temporary feeding.

Later these containers can be used for storage or cleanup. Rubbermaid also makes 100-, 150- and 300-gallon stock tanks that make excellent feeders and water units for permanent use.

Wild horses do not understand that bedding straw and shavings are not food. Although eating bedding straw will not harm the horse, it will produce a feeling of fullness and thus he may not eat more nutritional feed. Wood shavings can cause impaction and serious problems.

COMMERCIAL BOARDING FACILITIES

If stabling at home is not possible, a commercial boarding facility may be an alternative. Some boarding facilities will not accept wild horses, and others have restrictions on accepting stallions, so you should check on these two matters first at the facility you are considering. Here are other questions you will want answered:

- What type of feed do they use? Many facilities feed hay cubes or alfalfa, which may not be the diet of choice for newly adopted wild horses.
- Are they willing to feed your horse a lower-protein hay, such as barley, oat, timothy or other grass-hay mix, until the horse can be gradually switched over to a higher-protein hay?
- How often do they feed? A wild horse needs to be fed a minimum of twice a day; smaller feedings three or four times a day are even better.
- What type of corral will your horse be kept in?
- Will they allow you to have exclusive use of a corral for your horse for an unlimited time?
- What type of shelter do they provide?
- What type of water system do they use?
- What fire prevention plan do they have?
- Do they have night lighting?
- Do they have round-the-clock caretakers?
- What kind of inoculations do they require?
- Do they require a regular worming program?
- Do they have a veterinarian on call?
- What will the trip charge be for your veterinarian to come to this facility?
- What do they charge per month? Extra charges?

When you have a list of several boarding facilities that sound good, visit them. Are they clean? Do the horses boarded there appear to be in good condition? Talk to people who board their horses at the facility. How far is the facility from your home?

TRANSPORTING YOUR HORSE HOME

Decide how you will transport your newly adopted wild horse from the adoption site to your home. If possible, arrangements should be made to use a four-horse or stock trailer. Trailers with partitions that run down the middle or length of the trailer can be a problem. A stock trailer with a center-cut gate (one that extends the width of the trailer) is preferable because the horse can be confined in an area large enough to turn around in but not so large that he can move to the back of the trailer while traveling. The trailer must be the step-in type, not a drop-ramp type, or it will not be accepted by the BLM. The floor of the trailer should be of nonskid material. You can change the surface of the flooring by putting sand or dirt on it.

A panicked wild horse may view a window in the front of the trailer as an avenue of escape. To prevent this, make an X with masking tape across the window. Also, you may want to put a small amount of hay in the trailer manger before the horse is loaded. This will keep the horse occupied during transport.

.3.

THE VETERINARIAN

Basic care for the newly adopted wild horse will start even before your horse arrives at your home or boarding facility.

It is important to find a veterinarian who is familiar with the special needs of a wild horse and willing to work with you to develop a health program designed for your horse. You should find a veterinarian *before* your horse arrives. It may be possible for your veterinarian to examine your horse at the adoption site, where restraining chutes and handlers are available. Although your veterinarian will not be able to give your horse a complete hands-on examination, by looking at the health record he or she will be able to determine whether your horse needs additional shots, worming or other medical attention, and to give you instructions concerning the horse's diet.

Check with the BLM official in charge of the adoption to coordinate loading your horse into the chute with the arrival of the veterinarian.

While a wild horse must rely on itself and other members of the herd when he is ill or injured, your adopted horse must depend on you. Actually, your veterinarian, your farrier and you will form a team of caregivers. Whom you choose and how you relate to your team are two of the most important elements in the care of your horse.

Communication between you and the veterinarian is essential. While your veterinarian has the medical knowledge and training to treat your animal, most likely you will be the first to recognize when your horse is ill, injured or just "off." With good communication, when you explain how your horse is acting and what you have observed, your veterinarian will be able to determine if medical care is needed or tell you what you should do. If you can't talk to each other, misunderstandings can occur that could lead to mistakes or even permanent injury to your horse. If you cannot communicate with your veterinarian, or if he or she is unwilling to answer your questions, find a veterinarian who will work with you. Don't be afraid to ask questions. There is no such thing as a stupid question.

Most veterinarians specialize in the treatment of specific types of animals, such as dogs and cats, birds, large animals or horses. Your best choice will be an equine veterinarian, who has probably chosen this specialty because of a special love and understanding of horses.

Talk to neighbors and other local residents who own horses. Find out which veterinarians they use. The telephone book will list veterinarians in your area. Also, the American Veterinary Medical Association (AVMA) will be able to give you the names of local equine veterinarians.

The receptionist at a veterinary clinic will be able to answer most questions you may have. You might want to ask:

- Is the veterinarian willing to treat a wild horse? (Some veterinarians won't treat wild horses or have negative feelings about them.)
- Is the veterinarian associated with a clinic or hospital? Some equine veterinarians operate out of mobile units only.
- Does the veterinarian have facilities for surgery and hospitalization? If not, what arrangements are made if this need arises? While some mobile veterinarians may have special arrangements with another veterinarian to use a facility for surgery, others may

have to refer you to another veterinarian for care that requires hospitalization. This should not be the only factor in determining your choice of a veterinarian, but it is important.

- Is the veterinarian on 24-hour call? Some veterinarians work only Monday through Friday or until 6:00 P.M. If the veterinarian is not on 24-hour call, is a referral veterinarian available? Many veterinarians just work "off" hours for other veterinarians.
- Will the veterinarian come to the horse, or will you have to take the horse to the clinic? While you can usually save money by transporting your horse to the clinic, in some instances, such as a leg injury, or if you don't have a trailer, it may be preferable for the veterinarian to come to you.
- What are the trip charges? Veterinarians usually charge a set fee per mile to come to the horse.
- Is there an additional charge for weekend, night or emergency calls?
- Does the veterinarian make calls in your area on specific days? Some veterinarians make all routine calls in a neighborhood, such as inoculations, worming and health checks, on a specific day. If such an arrangement doesn't already exist, you may be able to arrange with the veterinarian and your neighbors for routine calls to be made on a specific day, with owners sharing the trip charge. Most veterinarians appreciate this consideration of their professional time.
- What are the veterinarian's charges for routine work, such as health check, inoculations and worming?
- How much notice does the veterinarian need in order to make a routine call? Some veterinarians are so busy that appointments must be made several weeks in advance.
- Does the veterinarian have a "well horse program"? A typical such one-year program includes a physical checkup every six months; four dewormings, if needed; two fecal flotation tests, to determine the presence of worms; inoculations; and teeth floated (trimmed), if needed. At the same time your veterinarian can recommend changes in diet, exercise and husbandry.
- How does the veterinarian want to be paid? Is payment to be made when the animal is treated, or can you establish an account? Does he or she accept credit cards? Can a payment plan be arranged in the event of serious injury or surgery?

• Would the veterinarian be willing to meet with you so you could get to know him or her personally? Veterinarians are very busy, but most would be willing to spend a few minutes speaking with you.

Once you have found several veterinarians in your area, spend a little time getting to know them. The one you feel most comfortable with, the one who is willing to answer your questions and is willing to teach you how to care for your horse, is probably your best choice.

There are many things you can do to make your veterinarian's visit a pleasant experience. When you know the veterinarian is coming, have your horse tied with a secure halter and lead rope. If this is not possible, as with a newly caught wild horse, at least have the horse confined to a small area. On hot days or in foul weather, a covered area will make examining your horse easier. A cross-tie pole to tie a reluctant horse will make the examination safer. Provide a clean bucket (for warm water) and paper towels. For night visits make sure that lighting is available. When you first put in your corral, it is a good idea to plan for the placement of night lights. In an emergency, car lights or even flashlights will do.

Discuss with your veterinarian how to take your animal's temperature, pulse, heart rate and respiration rate. Other how-to information, such as listening for gut sounds, will be a part of your education. Your veterinarian should be willing to teach you these basics of husbandry.

Ask your veterinarian what equipment, such as a thermometer, bandages, wound medications, disinfectants or antiseptics, you should have in a first aid kit designed for your horse. Your veterinarian may have other suggestions or substitutions for the first aid kit items listed below:

Nitrofurazone solution or dressing
Ichthammol ointment 20%
Granulex V or other proud flesh treatment
Betadine solution
iodine tincture
Blood Stop Powder
Novasan, Roccal-D or other disinfectant

mineral oil
stethoscope
needle holder or instrument for removing splinters
equine thermometer
humane horse twitch
hoof pick
bandage scissors
cotton roll
Kling gauze
Vetrap
gauze sponges
quilted leg wrap
tape
Kopertox

It is important to learn how to use these medications and supplies properly. Some, such as Betadine solution, while satisfactory for wound cleaning, can be very damaging to the eye.

Talking to your veterinarian and discussing how he or she likes to do things will make your horse's medical care a pleasant experience.

The following chart can be used as a reference guide. Whether for routine calls or emergencies, a written record is an advantage for health care. When the veterinarian comes for a checkup, he or she can more easily determine which vaccinations and worming medications your horse needs. Also, being aware of the horse's normal vital signs can help detect an oncoming problem if the signs deviate from normal.

MEDICAL RECORD

Name _____ Sex _____ Age _____ Color _____
Capture Area _____ State _____
Capture Date _____ Adoption Date _____
Freeze Brand No. __ __ __ __ __ __ __
Signalment Key _____ BLM ID. No. _____
BLM Regional Office Telephone (____) _____
Veterinarian's Name _____
Telephone (____) _____

FIRST EXAMINATION:

Date _____

Veterinarian's Diet Recommendations: _____
_____
_____
_____
_____

☐ Worming Products _____
☐ Vaccinations
☐ Eastern Equine Encephalomyelitis
☐ Western Equine Encephalomyelitis
☐ Venezuelan Equine Encephalomyelitis
☐ Influenza or Shipping Fever
☐ Tetanus
☐ Rhinopneumonitis
☐ *Streptococcus equi* (Strangles or Distemper)
Recommendations to buy for First-Aid Kit: _____
_____
_____
_____
_____

NORMAL VITAL SIGNS (at rest)

Temperature _____
Heart Rate _____
Respiration Rate _____
Pulse _____

NEXT VISIT: _____

NOTES: _____
_____
_____
_____

.4.

YOUR HORSE'S HEALTH

L et's face it, newly adopted wild horses usually look like something between a hairy whatchamacallit and a poorly cared for domestic horse. But underneath is a beautiful sleek animal you will be proud to own and ride.

What your horse looks like will depend greatly on the condition he was in when he came off the range. Winter is extremely hard on wild horses, and even those living on the best ranges will show a marked decrease in weight and condition during this time of year.

Horses caught during the first part of the roundup season will have had a better opportunity to eat high-quality feed at the BLM holding facilities before the beginning of the adoption season. It is not uncommon for a horse to gain as much as 75 to 150 pounds from the time of capture to the time of adoption.

In the wild, of course, horses have no barns or warm winter blankets. Psychologically wild horses need a clear view in all directions and will avoid even the shelter of a grove of trees, so nature provides the horses with thick coats that are often 3 to 4 inches long. About the time of year that the adoptions are held, the horses are shedding their winter coats and unfortunately look like moth-eaten creatures with large handfuls of hair falling out.

Any assessment of your horse's health begins by just looking at the horse. Knowing how your horse looks and acts when he is healthy is important in being able to judge whether he is ill or injured. You won't be able to do some of the following informal examinations until your horse is gentled and will allow you to put your hands on him, but it is a good idea to know what to look for.

Healthy coat   A horse in good condition has a full coat with a slight to high sheen. White, gray and some roan coats are less reflective than bay, sorrel and black coats and therefore shine less. The hairs of the coat should lie down smoothly. When a horse is ill, the muscles in the skin tend to pull the hairs upright, the same way people experience goose pimples when they are ill.

Resting   Although horses often rest one leg, usually a hind leg, by rolling it forward to the edge of the hoof, a healthy horse alternates the resting leg. If a horse always rests the same leg, there may be a medical reason. Horses can and do sleep while standing by locking their patella, or kneecap, into a position that holds the leg rigid while sleeping. Healthy horses who feel secure will lie down, either by folding their legs under them or lying flat. But if the horse contnues to lie down when you approach, is unable or unwilling to rise or lies down as soon as you leave, then something is wrong.

Changes in behavior   If your horse is usually a hearty eater and becomes reluctant to eat, is usually nervous and becomes quiet or vice versa, is standing with his head in a lowered position or exhibits other changes in normal behavior, you should look for additional signs of illness or injury.

Breathing   Count each time the horse breathes in (inhales) or out (exhales), but not both. A healthy horse at rest should breathe between 8 and 16 times per minute. A large horse will breathe fewer times a minute while a smaller horse, pony or foal will breathe more often. A horse that is overweight, pregnant or overheated may also have a higher respiration rate. If your horse is breathing faster than 20 times per minute and is not being stressed, overheated or exercised, there may be something wrong. You should not be able to hear rattling, congestion or coughing. These symptoms of health problems should be reported to your veterinarian.

Heart rate   At rest, a foal that's two to four weeks old will have a normal heart rate of between 70 and 90 beats per minute. At six to twelve months old the average is 45 to 60 beats per minute, while a horse two to three years old will average 35 to 45 beats per minute. Exercise, excitement, hot weather and other factors can raise normal heart rate, but a heart rate of more than 45 beats per minute should be considered abnormal, especially if the horse is showing any other signs of abnormal behavior. The average horse usually has three heartbeats for every breath.

Temperature   Normal temperature for the horse at rest is approximately 99.5 to 101.4 degrees F, although foals or young horses may be slightly higher at 102 degrees F. When your horse is gentle enough to allow you to handle his tail, it is a good idea to have your veterinarian show you how to take your horse's temperature.

Manure   A normal adult horse will pass 30 to 40 pounds of fecal waste product per day, in an average of ten separate movements. Depending on the type of feed, the color of the manure will be yellow-greenish to brown. Oat hay may produce a brown color, while alfalfa produces green droppings. Droppings should be firm enough to hold shape but not hard. Hard droppings may indicate a lack of water, poor feed, constipation or lack of exercise. Soft droppings may be caused by a feed or grass that's too green, too much bran or digestive tract problems. It is not unusual for a horse to have a loose bowel movement while you are first training. This is from nerves and should not cause concern. Diarrhea should be noted for color and the presence of mucus or blood, and reported to your veterinarian. Mucus-covered feces, with or without an unpleasant odor, can indicate too little roughage or too much grain. Although some grain can be expected to pass through the digestive system whole, large amounts of unchewed grain can indicate problems with teeth.

Urine   Normal urine may be clear, whitish, yellow or reddish-yellow, transparent or cloudy. It should not have a sharp or foul smell, have any lumps or clots, be dark red or brown in color or show any signs of blood. Any of these signs or changes in what is normal for your horse should be reported to your veterinarian immediately.

Vaginal discharge   During a mare's heat (estrus) cycle white, straw-colored or slightly pinkish discharge may stain her hind legs. Any continuous, thick, greenish-yellow discharge, foul odor or loss of hair on the hind legs should be reported to your veterinarian immediately.

Appetite   Changes in your horse's appetite should be watched. Eating lightly at a single feeding should not be cause for alarm, but if lack of appetite continues at other feedings it should be reported to your veterinarian.

Mucous membranes   The nostrils, mouth, eyelids, anus, prepuce and vagina are all mucous membranes and should normally be salmon-pink in color. The eyelids and mouth are easiest to check. Should the color be pale or yellow, bluish, purplish or dark red, report this to your veterinarian.

Gut sounds   A healthy horse will always have intestinal sounds made from natural gases passing through the liquid and solid contents of the digestive tract. A stethoscope will come in handy, but you can hear these sounds by placing your ear on the horse's stomach area. Listen on both sides. Lack of sound, which may indicate impaction or other colic problems, should be reported to your veterinarian. It is a good idea to listen to these sounds at different times until you know what your horse's digestion normally sounds like.

All horses adopted from the BLM Adopt-A-Horse program are wormed and given vaccinations against the major equine diseases. Most of the vaccinations need to be administered in multiple doses—the initial inoculation plus one or two boosters—within a specific time frame in order to be effective; a single booster dose is then given yearly for continued protection. High-risk horses, such as those at a boarding facility and show horses, may require some vaccinations more frequently; check with your veterinarian.

Some of the horses in the BLM program have not received booster shots within the suggested time frame; as a result, they may have less effective protection or their vaccinations may be invalid. It is important to have your veterinarian check the health record you're given at the time of adoption for validity of vaccinations. Part or all of series may have to be readministered.

INTERNAL PARASITES

Internal parasites, or worms, have little respect for a horse's breed, age, size or lineage. From very young foals to the "senior citizen" group, from horses of unknown parentage to renowned "blue bloods," worms take an enormous toll.

No other condition produces such an extensive list of symptoms in horses. The presence of worms is evidenced by one or more of the following signs:

- Dull, listless appearance
- Dry, rough hair coat
- Skin conditions (for example, sores)
- Incomplete shedding
- Erratic appetite or lack of appetite
- Loss of weight
- Diarrhea or other bowel disorders
- Colic
- Lack of or slow growth, sometimes as much as 30 percent less than in worm-free horses
- Anemia or other blood abnormalities
- Loss of ambition and ability to perform

Also "hardkeepers," horses that do not do well even when they have good feed and are in general good health. They may have a parasite infestation.

Among the many types of internal parasites, the most common are large and small strongyles, ascarids, bot flies and pinworms. A fifth type, lungworms, is found in wild horses that have had contact with burros. Since almost every wild horse has had such contact, directly or indirectly, it is important to remind your veterinarian that your wild horse should be treated for this type of parasite also.

Strongyles

Large and small strongyles are by far the most damaging and destructive to the horse of any of the five groups of parasites.

Approximately forty species of strongyles are less than an inch long and are referred to as small strongyles. Three other species of large strongyles may be as long as 2 inches. Parasites in the large strongyle group—often called bloodworms, redworms or palisade worms—cause the most severe and destructive effect.

These parasites live mostly in the cecum (blind gut) and large bowel. The adults, found in great numbers, attach themselves to the intestinal wall to feed from the horse's blood. When an animal serves as host for hundreds or thousands of these blood suckers, it is little wonder that he becomes anemic, a hard keeper and a poor performer.

Strongyles do not confine their activities to blood sucking. The larvae, or immature forms, of these species (*Strongylus vulgaris*) are adventuresome troublemakers, working their way through the intestinal wall and into the blood vessels.

These nomads of the bloodstream hitchhike to various organs, including the liver, heart and lungs. In the course of their migrations, the larvae of *S. vulgaris* destroy healthy tissues and attach themselves to the walls of the mesenteric artery or its branches.

Any disturbance of the mesenteric artery, one of the main lines of blood supply to the intestines, is serious. As the larvae become firmly entrenched, the vessel walls weaken from the burden, and saclike pouches develop. Such a pouch, called an aneurysm, fills with blood that cannot circulate. These weakened areas sometimes rupture, causing hemorrhage and the death of the horse.

More frequently, clots of blood that break away from the aneurysm become free-floating chunks that lodge in smaller arteries and impede blood supply. Occasionally, a vessel becomes completely blocked, which results in the death of the tissue or organ deprived of such blood. Such blockages account for a type of colic in horses that is often fatal. It is believed that the majority of cases of colic result from the disturbance of the bloodstream by the larvae of strongyles.

Ascarids

The ascarid, or common roundworm, is quite at home in the small intestine of the horse. It is a large white worm, often the diameter of a lead pencil and some 8 to 15 inches in length. Ascarids exact a high cost in terms of poor condition, stunted growth and even death.

Ascarids are seldom a problem in domestic horses older than four to five years, but wild horses may have not developed an immunity to these parasites and may be more susceptible to infestation at any age. Infective eggs are swallowed in the course of eating contaminated grass or bedding and drinking egg-polluted water. Soon after ingestion, the eggs hatch and the larvae are freed into the small intestine. After leaving the eggs, the larvae rapidly penetrate the intestinal wall and are taken by the bloodstream to the liver.

After they have devastated the liver tissue, the larvae once again enter the bloodstream and travel to the lung. They migrate through the lung tissue and enter the air passage. Helped along by an occasional cough, the larvae make their way up the trachea to the throat, where they are reswallowed. They then grow to maturity in the small intestine.

Heavily infested foals cough and are subject to fever, pneumonia and other debilitating effects of the migrating ascarid larvae. Further, because of the large size of the adult worm and the great numbers that can be involved, the intestine may become partially or even completely obstructed, producing colic that can terminate in death.

Bot Flies

In the late summer months the bot fly, or nit fly, is the horse's number one enemy. The continual annoyance caused by the bot fly buzzing around the horse's head and legs is a source of nervous frustration to the animal and agitation to the horseman.

The bot fly deposits eggs on the hair around the chin and on the legs of the horse. These eggs are ready to hatch after about seven days. However, hatching does not take place until the eggs are rubbed by the warm, moist lips of the horse. The eggs, or nits, may lie on the hair for as long as two months awaiting this stimulus.

The liberated embryos cling to the lips and gums and soon start an active life. Burrowing through the gums, the tongue or other adjacent tissue, the tiny bot moves toward its home, the stomach. In countless numbers, the bots become firmly attached to the stomach wall to feed and grow. Mature bots are about three-quarters of an inch long and very plump.

After eight to eleven months of living at the expense of the horse, the bot worms are passed in the droppings. Upon reaching the outside world, the bot worms undergo transformation and become bot flies.

Besides draining the horse's strength and nourishment, the bot leaves the stomach inflamed and ulcerated, so that the horse is subject to indigestion or infection. Infestation with bots can be great enough to interfere with digestive processes and the passage of food from the stomach.

Pinworms

Pinworms are seen around the rectum and in the droppings. Of considerable irritation to the horse, pinworms provoke a lot of tail rubbing and itching of the surrounding area. Although they are less damaging to the system than the parasite groups considered above, the constant annoyance, irritation and loss of tail hair from rubbing affects the peace of mind, actions and appearance of the horse.

Lungworms

Although as many as 25 percent to 100 percent of adult burros are infested with lungworms, they rarely cause problems for the burro. In the horse, however, the larvae can cause coughing and lung damage. In the horse, the larvae may never mature to adult worms but instead remain in the lungs for various lengths of time.

The lungworm larvae are picked up from pasture during the summer months as they migrate to the lungs, where the adult worm remains. Eggs from the lungs pass up to the horse's throat and are then swallowed. Some eggs are then passed out with feces onto the pasture. Because some horses infested with lungworm do not pass lungworm eggs in the feces, worm egg counts are not reliable in diagnosing their presence.

For a horse with bots in the stomach, ascarids in the small intestines, strongyles in the large intestine, pinworms in the rectum and lungworms in the lungs, the fight for survival is perpetual and costly.

Your horse may harbor as many as fifty-seven species of internal parasites. It is essential for his health that you work with your veterinarian to plan a program for parasite control. Good parasite-control measures include:

Proper manure disposal   It is advisable to compost stable manure before spreading it on pasture. In small corrals and pasture lots, it is important to pick up all manure and compost at least every other day.

Pasture   Mow and chain harrow the pasture frequently. Avoid overstocking. When possible, rotate use of the pasture with other species. Graze weanlings and yearlings separate from other horses.

Feed   Use feeders for hay and grain, and keep all feed from contact with feces.

Deworming   Consult your veterinarian as soon as possible to determine what's best for your horse. It is advisable to worm all horses on the property at the same time, quarantine newcomers or transients and have your veterinarian conduct periodic fecal examinations.

Fly control   Care must be taken with newly adopted horses and the use of chemical repellents. Spaulding Laboratories have developed organic methods, such as fly predators (beneficial insects) that lay their eggs in the fly pupa and prevent it from developing. This treatment is harmless to other living things and is highly recommended.

Wild horses or those in poor condition sometimes have problems taking the full dosage of some worming products. The following worming program has been used at the LIFE Equine Center with excellent results: As soon as the horse is accepting grain, pelleted feed or other supplements, Strongid C worming pellets are added as a top dressing to daily feed for a period of thirty days or until the horse is able to be handled. This medication is less severe than a single-dose wormer and removes parasites in a more gradual way. As soon as the horse can be handled easily and safely by a veterinarian, Dryex T. F. is administered by stomach tube. Your veterinarian will then recommend a continuing health program for your horse.

MAJOR HORSE DISEASES

Distemper

Strangles, or distemper, is a contagious disease caused by the baterial organism *Streptococcus equi*. The most common method of transmission is through contact with other horses, contaminated equipment and feed and water troughs. Generally speaking, it is an upper respiratory infection involving the nose, pharynx, sinuses and glands of the head and neck area. Symptoms of strangles include a rise in temperature, difficulty in breathing and an increased respiratory rate, nasal discharge, restlessness and a lack of appetite. These symptoms are followed by a swelling of the lymph nodes of the head and throat region; the swollen lymph nodes may ab-

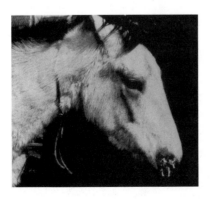

A HORSE WITH STRANGLES. A RUNNY NOSE USUALLY INDICATES AN UPPER RESPIRATORY INFECTION. (PHOTO BY BARBARA EUSTIS-CROSS)

scess, rupture and discharge an infectious, puslike material. If infection spreads to other tissues and organs, the result can be chronic infection or death. With proper care and management, the infection can remain localized in the tissues of the head and upper neck, and secondary complications or death from suffocation can be avoided.

The severity of the disease may be greatly increased by factors producing stress and lowered resistance, such as fatigue, parasitism, hauling in open trucks and exposure to severe weather, or by concurrent viral infections.

During an outbreak, strict sanitary measures are needed to prevent spread of the infection to other horses. Common feed boxes or watering troughs should not be used. Stables, watering devices, feed buckets, halters, ropes and other equipment should be cleaned with diluted Nolvasan.

For a complete recovery it is essential that you work with your veterinarian to provide your horse the best possible medical care.

Equine Influenza

Equine influenza is a highly contagious virus disease known to be caused by two distinct strains identified individually as Equine A-1 and Equine A-2. This disease occurs in susceptible horses of all ages, producing what is commonly termed "the flu" or "two-year-old cough." The two viruses produce clinically identical patterns of disease. Immunity produced as a result of infection with one of the virus strains does not provide protection against the other strain. For that reason it is important that your horse be vaccinated against both diseases.

Equine influenza appears suddenly. Sick horses show a temperature rise, respiratory symptoms and loss of appetite, and are depressed. Signs of muscular weakness and tremors are common. In some cases there may be swelling of the lower surface extremities accompanied by inflammation of the tendon sheaths. A watery nasal discharge may later change to a thick yellowish one. At times the lymph glands of the head and neck may become swollen, making it difficult to distinguish this disease from strangles.

Fatalities from the flu are rare, provided the horses is kept at complete rest and the disease does not become complicated by bacterial infection. The usual complications from the secondary bacterial infections are inflammation of the mucous membrane of the nose, the larynx, the pharynx, and the trachea; pneumonia; and digestive disturbances. Prolonged cases of pneumonia may be complicated further by toxic effects on the heart, liver and kidneys. Failure to provide an adequate rest period during and following the disease appears to be the principal cause of the persistence of symptoms and chronic coughing.

As with any disease outbreak, the horse should be separated from other animals, and feed boxes, watering troughs and other equipment should be cleaned with diluted Nolvasan.

Rhinopneumonitis

Rhinopneumonitis, otherwise known as contagious abortion or EHV-1 infection, is an equine respiratory disease caused by a herpes virus similar to the one that causes the common cold in humans. Rhinopneumonitis has some characteristics of the human cold and is often called a "cold." An acute and highly contagious disease characterized by respiratory infection in horses and abortion in pregnant mares, it often causes a fatal broncho-pneumonia. One form of the infection produces ataxia (a lack of muscular coordination), paresis (partial paralysis), paralysis and death.

The virus may survive from four to seven weeks when dried on horsehair or blankets. It is present in nasal excretions, saliva and blood, and possibly in the feces during the acute period. It is abundant in the fetal membranes and fluids and in all tissues of an aborted fetus, and it may also spread by contaminated feed, water and other items used around the stable. Recovered animals continue to harbor and intermittently shed the virus to others. Immunity as a result of infection is short-lived, after which the recovered animal is again susceptible.

Tetanus

Tetanus, or lockjaw as it is commonly called, is a toxemia caused by the organism *Clostridium tetani*, which lives in the intestinal tract of horses and is found in large quantities in equine feces. It is characterized by stiffness of any or all of the animal's muscles. In the advanced stages, the reflexes are increased and the animal is easily frightened into violent spasms by sudden movement or noise. Spasms in the muscles of the head cause difficulty in chewing. Ears become erect, legs and tail become stiff and sweating and high fever occur. Death may finally result from asphyxiation caused by spasms of muscles controlling respiration.

Infection

Infections occur as a result of contaminated wounds. Puncture wounds are the most serious, but any wound contaminated with foreign matter (such as harness and saddle galls, lacerations from barbed wire or puncture wounds from dropped nails or other objects) may result in fatal tetanus infection.

Encephalomyelitis

Encephalomyelitis, commonly called sleeping sickness, blind staggers or brain fever, is an acute viral disease of birds and mammals, including man, horses, ponies and mules. It is characterized by central nervous disturbances and is often fatal.

Signs of the disease include high fever, partial loss of vision, reeling gait, lack of coordination, yawning, grinding of teeth, drowsiness, sagging lower lip and inability to swallow. In the later stages, horses are unable to rise, become paralyzed and die. Death occurs in about 50 percent of cases. Horses that do not die may be permanently affected by nerve damage from the virus. Since the disease is easily confused with rabies, moldy-corn poisoning and various heavy-metal poisonings, it is imperative that you consult a qualified veterinarian for a positive diagnosis.

Encephalomyelitis usually occurs from June to November (or the appearance of the first frost). The virus is transmitted by mosquitoes from birds to horses. The resulting infection may lead to disease of the brain and spinal cord.

The two most common strains of the virus are the Western type and the Eastern type; the Western type affords no immunity against the Eastern type and vice versa. Because neither the Eastern nor Western strain is geographically restricted, horses must be vaccinated against both types. A third virus strain called Venezuelan is seen in horses from such border states as Texas, New Mexico, Arizona and California.

A LIFE Foundation study in 1988 revealed that almost 90 percent of wild horses develop an unspecified upper respiratory cough, sometimes with accompanying runny nose. In most horses it will run its course in one to three weeks with or without treatment. It is generally felt that this cough arises from rapid changes in climate, diet and stress. But, as with any upper respiratory problem, it needs to be watched closely.

If your newly adopted horse shows any of the following signs, contact your veterinarian immediately:

- Not eating all his feed or weight loss
- Depressed or standing with head hanging low
- Difficulty breathing or rapid breathing
- Coughing

RINGWORM

Ringworm is caused not by a parasite or worm but by a fungus that attacks the skin and lives in the hair follicles. Tiny spores form a chain around the hair shaft. As the hair become brittle and breaks, the fungus spreads outward, leaving a round ring.

WILD HORSES HAVE BEEN THROUGH A LOT OF STRESS, SO DON'T EXPECT THEM TO LOOK THEIR BEST! WITH TIME AND CARE THEY WILL SOON LOOK MUCH BETTER. THE HORSE IN THE MIDDLE WITH THE STRIPE, DELTA, APPEARS IN MANY PHOTOS THROUGHOUT THE BOOK. THIS WAS TAKEN THE DAY SHE WAS ADOPTED.

THE HORSE IN THE BACKGROUND EXHIBITS SYMPTOMS OF RINGWORM.

Ringworm is contagious to humans and should be treated by a veterinarian. However, it usually is treated fairly easily and without it spreading to the adopters or other animals. If you think your horse may have this problem, separate it from other animals. Until the veterinarian can diagnose and begin treatment, be sure to wash your hands after touching the horse or any equipment it has been in contact with.

COLIC

Colic is a general term used to describe any abdominal pain. Probably unknown to the wild horse in its natural environment, colic is the number one killer of domestic horses in the United

States. Feeding the horse unnatural feeds on an artificial schedule, overfeeding, an irregular feeding schedule, feeding moldy feeds, changing diet too fast, the stress of confinement, lack of exercise or overwork, feeding before a hard workout, feeding too soon after a workout, parasitism and digestion of sand or other foreign materials are only some of the reasons for colic in captive horses. A horse with colic may show some or all of the following signs:

- Lack of appetite
- Marked personality change
- Dull or lethargic attitude
- Groaning or sighing
- Kicking at the belly with the hindfoot
- Pawing at the ground
- Looking at the flank
- Cocking or resting one back foot and then the other in a restless manner
- Lying down and getting up repeatedly
- Lying on the back with legs pulled into the stomach
- Rolling in a thrashing manner
- Switching or pumping tail
- Walking in a circle
- Standing as though attempting to urinate but without results
- Unable to pass feces or diarrhea
- Sweating
- Grinding teeth

If your horse is showing one or more of these signs, *immediately* call your veterinarian. A simple colic can turn into a death warrant in a remarkably short time. Your veterinarian will advise you what to do until he or she arrives.

Wild horses are remarkably tolerant to human error and, with sound animal husbandry practices, regular worming and yearly booster inoculations, they are easy keepers once they have adjusted to captivity. With strong legs and hooves that put domestic horses to shame, they seldom develop leg or hoof problems.

Find out if your veterinarian has lecture clinics or if a local humane society or college offers classes in horse care.

.5.

FOALS AND FOALING

If you adopt a mare over the age of two there will be a possibility that she is in foal. Unless the mare is gentle and calm enough to allow your veterinarian to confirm pregnancy by a rectal palpation examination or a blood test, the best plan is to be prepared. You will be preparing for an event that may not happen, but knowing what to expect and how to deal with it can prevent problems later.

Your veterinarian may recommend additional or special inoculations for a mare who may be pregnant. Additionally, he or she may have diet recommendations for before and after foaling; care procedures for before, during and after birth; and instructions for foal care, such as treating the umbilical cord, antibiotic injections and other care, depending on your skill and the gentleness of the mare. You will want to understand these recommendations completely before the birth. Write them down!

As you read this chapter, remember that you will need to consider how tame your mare is at every step of the way. If something is recommended that will cause her undue stress or make her nervous, do not proceed. Talk to your veterinarian and discuss an alternate plan.

MARE AND FOAL.

Mares usually deliver between 330 and 350 days after conceiving, although any time between eleven months and twelve months is within the normal range. Because most wild horses foal between January and early July, watch a newly adopted mare especially carefully during these months.

Your horse may not show signs of pregnancy until a few weeks or even days before delivery, but there are signs you can look for. Your horse may show all of the signs, just a few or none at all. Most mares' udders become enlarged during the last two to four weeks before foaling, although some young mares have udders that fill and then become small again throughout the pregnancy. Others do not show any udder development until after the foal is born and are still able to provide ample milk for the foal.

Four to six days before foaling, the nipples may begin to fill and become rounder. Two to three days prior to delivery, most mares secrete a thick, yellowish wax from the nipples. Occasionally, milk will drip or even stream from the nipples before foaling. This first milk is actually colostrum, which contains protective antibodies the foal needs to receive during the first twelve to eighteen hours after birth. It is important that you let your veterinarian know if this happens because the mare may be losing important colostrum.

THE BIRTH

First-stage labor occurs about twelve hours before birth. The mare may become restless, be off her feed, act as if she has a stomach ache, sweat in odd patches or all over, raise her tail to urinate small amounts and/or frequently get up and down. Your mare may show all, some or none of the above signs. If you do see signs of the first stage of labor, this is usually a good time to call your veterinarian to warn him or her and to get any last-minute instructions. Have paper and pencil ready to make notes.

It is important to allow your mare as much privacy as possible. A wild mare in her natural environment will leave the herd to foal and not return for one or more days. Even then she will keep the foal away from the majority of herd members until it is stronger. If your mare feels threatened or "on display," she may become defensive, dangerously delay foaling or even reject the foal.

During the second stage of labor the mare's waters will break. The water will be a clear to slightly yellowish or brownish, thickened or mucus-type fluid. This fluid may be released all at once or, if there is only a small hole in the placenta, in a gradual drip. At this point the mare may relax, eat and drink. Some mares will lick at the amniotic fluid; this is normal and should not be prevented. Birth usually occurs within an hour after the waters break.

During third-stage labor, the mare will have strong contractions that can be seen by the observer. Usually mares lie down during this time, although a few will remain standing. Most mares deliver the foal within twenty to sixty minutes. Usually one foot and then the other will appear, or both feet may appear together. The nose should appear resting on the legs. The mare may relax for a few minutes at this point. During normal delivery a few more contractions should expel the foal.

If the mare strains for more than twenty minutes without visible results, or if you see only one foot, two feet and no head, a head and no feet, or two hind feet, call your veterinarian *immediately*. He or she will give you instructions on what to do until medical help arrives. Your veterinarian may advise you to get the mare up and walking until he or she arrives.

THE FIRST HOURS OF LIFE

Once the foal's front feet, head and shoulders are visible, it may rest for a few minutes. When the foal is completely free of the mare, it will spend some time struggling to be free of the placenta. This is normal and helps the foal breath harder and expel any remaining fluid in the lungs.

Do not rush the mare into getting up, and do not disturb her at this point. The foal is still attached to the umbilical cord; as much as one-third of the foal's blood volume is still in the placenta and draining into the foal. The umbilical cord usually breaks naturally when the mare stands.

Generally the mare will begin licking the foal. Some wild mares will bite or paw at the newborn to encourage it to get up. This appears to be a survival instinct in wild horses and not an aggressive action as it would be in domestic horses. The foal should stand within two hours and nurse within six hours. This time is critical for the mare and foal to bond together; any disturbance from you could inhibit this natural bonding and could cause the mare to reject the foal. Do not bother cleaning up or removing the placenta until the foal is standing, has nursed and has spent some time getting to know its mother.

Within six hours the mare should pass the placenta membranes, or afterbirth. Your veterinarian will want to examine the afterbirth, so lay it aside for later. Even if the birth appears normal, it is important to have your veterinarian examine the mare and foal within twenty-four hours after birth.

It is a good idea to observe the mare from a distance until she has accepted the foal and it has nursed. If the mare appears nervous, you may need to back off further or leave her completely alone with the foal for an hour or two before checking back.

If the foal has not nursed within three hours, there may be a problem. If the mare appears to move away from the foal when it comes near, you may need to secure the mare by tying her head or hand-holding her while the foal begins to nurse. If the mare is not tame enough to allow you to do this, you should contact your veterinarian beforehand for instructions.

If the mare will stand with the foal but moves away when it tries to nurse, the mare's udder may be overfull or sensitive to touch. If the udder appears full and the mare will allow, you may try gently squeezing the nipple, pulling slightly and repeating until some of the milk is drained off and she is more comfortable. She may then allow the foal to nurse.

Some mares have large udders and/or small nipples, and the foal may have difficulty in nursing. If the mare will allow, have one person hold the mare while a helper squeezes out a few drops of milk and spreads it around the nipple. The helper should face the foal's head and use his or her body to gently move the foal close to the mare. Then, using the hand farthest from the mare and foal, guide the foal's mouth to the nipple by putting a hand under the jaw, while placing the thumb or index finger in the side of the foal's mouth. As the foal's mouth touches the nipple, apply a little pressure and wiggle the finger in the foal's mouth. The foal should show a sucking reflex by curling its tongue in a funnel and open its mouth enough for you to place it around the nipple. Squeezing a little milk into the foal's mouth may encourage the foal to suck. It is easier than it sounds, but don't get discouraged if you don't get results the first time.

If you have tried to help the foal nurse and it still has not nursed within four hours, call your veterinarian, who may want to immediately check the mare and foal for problems such as illness or congenital defects. The veterinarian may give the mare a tranquilizer, injections to increase milk production or other medical treatment. Calling the veterinarian at this point means you will be able to make plans or get instructions to make sure the foal is cared for properly.

THE IMPORTANCE OF COLOSTRUM

The mare's first milk is called colostrum. This milk contains about five times the protein of later milk, twice the energy concentration, high levels of vitamin A, a laxative that promotes the first bowel movement and high concentrates of antibodies that help protect the foal. The foal must receive colostrum within twelve to eighteen hours after birth. After that time the digestive tract changes and the antibodies cannot be absorbed. A foal will not develop its autoimmune system until it is two to three months old. The failure to receive these colostrum antibiotics is often cited as the primary factor in the death of newborn horses. It is important that you *do not give the foal any milk product or milk replacer until after the foal has received the colostrum.*

If the foal does not receive the colostrum by nursing, your veterinarian may advise you to milk the mare, if possible, and bottle-feed the colostrum to the foal. Your veterinarian will determine how much colostrum your foal will need.

The veterinarian may determine that the mare is unable to provide colostrum and will try to provide colostrum from another mare, a horse nursery, or a freeze-dried bank. The veterinarian will provide specific instructions on how to feed the foal.

THE ORPHAN OR EARLY WEANED FOAL

Although orphan foals are rare when wild horses are not under stress, some foals born in captivity are premature and require special care. Premature foals born four weeks or more before term are usually undersized and have soft, silky hair; they may have difficulty standing. The body temperature of these foals is usually 2 or 3 degrees below normal (normal temperature is 99.5 to 101.4 degrees F or even 102 in foals). Foals born two to three weeks before term may be of normal size but appear exceptionally thin and have a long, scrubby coat; they can usually stand with little or no help. Your veterinarian will help you determine if your foal is premature and give you any special instructions or medications the foal may need.

If the veterinarian determines that the foal should be separated from the mare, you may need to provide special housing and additional heat. It is important that the foal be housed inside at night, whenever possible. A barn stall is the best housing for a new orphan, but several inexpensive substitutes can be made with a little effort. A garage or other structure may be suitable for night-time housing if it is carefully prepared to prevent accidents. If the foal is housed on concrete, lay down several layers of newspaper and then a straw bedding to protect the foal from hard, cold flooring. One woman successfully raised her orphan foal Casino by keeping it in the kitchen at night! If inside housing is not possible, a tent covering the top of a small outdoor corral will help; you should place carpeting over the rails to about 4½ feet to help protect from drafts.

An economical foal pen can be made by laying out a square of baled hay approximately 10 feet by 10 feet. You can create a "hay corral" by staggering each row to create a secure wall that will protect the foal from drafts. As the foal grows older it will nibble at the hay, a good indication that it is ready for solid food. When the foal is old enough for a regular corral, the hay can be used for feed.

If your veterinarian determines that your foal needs it, additional heat can be provided by overhead heat lamps or a heat mat, although it is important that the pen be large enough so that the foal can leave the heated area. An excellent overhead heater is made by Merco. A separate control unit may be purchased for temperature control. Depending on size, units weigh between 6 and 11 pounds and require a sturdy horizontal rafter to attach the heater approximately 66 inches above the floor. You may also need to purchase an extension cord, as the cord that comes with the unit is only 6 feet long. One advantage of this type of heating is that you can use a straw bed for the foal's comfort. Kane Manufacturing makes an electronically heated fiberglass mat that was designed for other animals but is proving highly successful with orphan foals. A separate rheostat can be purchased for finer heat control. The direct heat on the foal's body appears to help it over-come minor stomach aches. Although straw beds may not be used with this type of heater, rubber mats such as those made by Linear appear to be a good substitute. Later these can be used in the bottom of trailers for better traction. Both types of heaters are used at the LIFE Equine Center.

The best method for feeding an orphan or early weaned foal depends on the age, condition and eating habits of the foal when it is orphaned. The following suggestions are general guidelines only. You and your veterinarian will have first-hand knowledge of your foal's needs and can best determine the most effective care for your orphan.

It is a good idea to take an orphan foal's temperature twice a day, morning and evening, until you have an average temperature as a guideline. Keep a clipboard, paper and pen near the foal's pen for notes concerning the feeding schedule, diet and veterinarian's directions. You will also want to keep track of how much the foal eats, its temperature and behavior and questions you want to ask the veterinarian.

Constipation is not uncommon in foals. If a foal does not defe-cate within twelve hours, it is probably constipated. This could develop into a serious condition and should be reported to your veterinarian.

Many foals have loose stools or diarrhea caused by diet adjust-ment, overfeeding, poor digestion or illness. The foal's digestive system may simply need time to adjust to homemade formulas or milk replacers, but diarrhea accompanied by a rise in temperature should be reported to your veterinarian *immediately*. Diarrhea with-out accompanying temperature should be reported to your veter-inarian if it doesn't stop within six hours.

If the foal develops diarrhea, it is important to cover the anal area and legs with a protective coating, such as petroleum jelly or the type of product that protects a human baby from diaper rash. In severe cases a coating of aloe vera gel under the petroleum jelly may be needed to soothe the area. Foals with diarrhea or consti-pation can benefit from doses of Equine Bene Bac Lactobacillus Paste (Borden) or Fastrack Non-runiment Paste (Conklin).

A foal naturally drinks only a few ounces at a time and may nurse 120 or more times per day. Feeding the foal infrequent, large meals

is often a strain on its digestive system and can result in cramps
and diarrhea. Infrequent feedings may also result in abnormal behavior and medical problems such as nursing on inanimate objects,
tongue sucking, rocking or ulcers.

Although foals can be taught to drink from a bucket, it is best
to start with bottle feeding. The sucking reflex creates saliva and
releases digestive enzymes. Lamb nipples, available from most feed
stores, seem to work best. Boiling the nipple first will soften the
rubber. Calf nipples are generally too large and hard, and the foal
may not suck on them. In an emergency, human baby bottles and
nipples will do, but try to find a long nipple.

Raising an orphan foal is not a one-person job. Work out a
schedule with family members (children, too), neighbors and
friends, especially during the first week. Most children will be
thrilled to help, and foals usually find children less threatening
than adults.

Some foals may be weak and unable to stand without assistance.
It is important that the foal stand to eat, even if someone must
hold it up. Soon the foal will understand that the food comes only
when it is standing and will make the extra effort to stand. Also,
with the foal in a standing position, there is less chance of the
formula going down the trachea and into the lungs.

The foal's mouth should be washed after feeding. Formula left
on the hair will cause it to break off. Although the hair will grow
back when the foal is removed from the formula, the unprotected
skin is unsightly, attracts flies and may become sensitive without
the hair coating.

It is important to groom the foal. An unused applicator mitt,
designed for applying coat dressings or fly repellents, makes a nice
grooming tool. It will conform to the foal's body and make it easy
to lightly massage the foal as you groom it. You may need to
stimulate the foal's urination and defecation by gently washing the
genital area after feeding. When the foal is unable to turn over, you
should turn it, alternating sides so it does not spend all of its time
resting on one side.

At the LIFE Equine Center, after the colostrum is given, orphan
foals are started on 8 ounces of LifeGuard (an electrolyte substitute
made by Smith-Kline Beecham), mixed according to directions.
This can be divided into two or more feedings over a period of

an hour. The next feeding should be given an hour later and consist of 4 ounces of LifeGuard with 4 ounces Borden's Foal-Lac mixed according to directions; this can also be divided into two feedings given within an hour. A third feeding of 8 ounces of Foal-Lac formula only is given one hour later. All formula mixtures should be approximately 98.6 degrees F (37 degrees C), or lukewarm to the touch. Leftover formula may be refrigerated and reheated for the next feeding; this should be the first bottle fed and should not be reheated more than once.

Within the first twenty-four hours the foal is given Borden's Equine Bene Bac Lactobacillus Paste or Conklin's Fastrack Non-runiment Paste, according to directions. If you have Fastrack Liquid, use ½ teaspoon per bottle.

During the first three days, the foals at the Equine Center are fed every hour from 6:00 A.M. to 10:00 P.M. They are checked at 2:00 A.M. and may be given an additional feeding then. A foal may not consume the entire ration at each feeding; unless the total intake is less than 128 ounces per twenty-four-hour period, don't be alarmed. The first day the foal may consume only 4 ounces or so per feeding. If the foal develops diarrhea, more frequent daytime feedings of four ounces each sometimes help.

On day four feedings may be reduced if the foal is eagerly finishing most of the formula at each feeding. By this time your records and observations will show how much the foal is willing to drink at one feeding. A single feeding should not be more than 24 ounces. At the Equine Center 31 percent of the foals needed sixteen feedings per day by day four, 8 percent needed twelve feedings, and 61 percent needed eight.

Bottle feeding can cause a foal to suck air; rubbing the stomach after feeding can help. Any time the formula, number of feedings or other dietary changes are made, watch the foal for signs of discomfort, constipation or diarrhea; report these to your veterinarian.

When the foal begins to nibble baled hay, or by the fifteenth day, a complete foal ration may be introduced. Start by placing ½ pound in a bucket placed about shoulder high to the foal. Add ½ ounce of Conklin's Fastrack Micro Feed per day or Borden's Equine Bene Bac Paste every three days. Remove any uneaten portion at the end of the day. Even though the feed will not spoil

FEEDING SCHEDULE

First feedings must be colostrum.

Age of foal	Foal-Lac oz. per feeding	No. of feedings per day	Total oz. per day	Foal-Lac Pellets & 16% Foal ration per day
1 bottle	8 LifeGuard	1–3	8	
1 bottle	4 LifeGuard +	1–3	4	
	4 Foal-Lac		4	
1 day	8	12–14	112–124	
2–3 days	8	16–18	128–140	none
4–14 days	16–24	8–16	140–192	none
15–21 days	24–32	6–8	196–209	½ lb. foal feed
22–28 days	24–32	6–8	196–209	½ lb. foal feed + 1 cup Foal-Lac Pellets
29–35 days	39–52	4–6	209–288	¾ lb. foal feed + 2 cups Foal-Lac Pellets
36–42 days	35–48	4	140–192	1 lb. foal feed + 3 cups Foal-Lac Pellets
43–49	25–48	4	140–192	1 lb. foal feed + 4 cups Foal-Lac Pellets
50–56	35–48	2	70–96	1½ lbs. foal feed + 5 cups Foal-Lac Pellets
2–3 mo.	Wean from liquid milk replacer.			2 lbs. foal feed + 6 cups Foal-Lac Pellets
3–4 mos.				3 lbs. foal feed + 6 cups Foal-Lac Pellets

in a single day, its high sugar content attracts flies. (You can give the uneaten portion to another horse rather than waste it.) If the foal is eating all the feed by midday, an additional ¼ pound of foal ration may be added to the diet. A clean bucket of fresh water and a mineralized salt block should be placed where the foal has free access to them. The foal should be stabilized at this point, and you should ask your veterinarian about a worming program and additional inoculations.

Now you can introduce the foal to bucket feeding. By this time the foal is acquainted with the smell and taste of the formula. Put about half the normal feeding in a 16-quart bucket. Dip your fingers in the formula and allow the foal to start sucking the formula from them. Slowly lower your fingers and the foal's mouth into the bucket, redipping the fingers as necessary. Soon the foal's mouth will be touching the formula. As he begins drinking, remove your fingers. When the foal finishes this formula, pour the remaining formula into the bucket and leave it with the foal. Remove any formula not consumed within an hour or two. Repeat this process at the next scheduled feeding.

Establish a permanent feeding station that allows the bucket to hang tipped slightly forward and about shoulder high to the foal. The bucket should be cleaned with warm soapy water and rinsed several times after each feeding. Be sure to continue regularly cleaning areas where formula spills on the foal's coat. During the first few days the foal may suck in air as it learns to drink, so watch for signs of cramping or discomfort. Contact your veterinarian if the foal appears uncomfortable. If it shows any signs of abnormal behavior, feed half the normal formula ration in the bucket, and several hours later feed the remaining formula with a bottle.

The feeding schedule presented on page 56 is based on the needs of a foal that will mature to approximately 800 to 1,000 pounds. To figure your foal's approximate adult size, add 100 to 200 pounds to the weight of the mother.

The above suggestions for feeding an orphan foal also apply to raising an orphan burro, but reduce the total amount of formula needed by approximately half. Also, orphan burros appear to require much more interaction with people or other animals than young horses do. At the LIFE Equine Center, orphan burros are raised for the first three weeks in a puppy pen in the staff living quarters. Amazingly, they do not challenge the barrier and seem content to watch what everyone is doing! Without this extra care, orphan burros seem to exhibit a higher incidence of abnormal behavior and medical problems such as ulcers. Close contact and support from your veterinarian is important in raising an orphan foal.

.6.

FEED

In its natural environment, the wild horse spends most of his time grazing on low-protein native grasses. This pattern of continually moving and eating is best suited to the equine digestive system. A wild horse on open range with good forage can choose different types of forage, which will provide the minerals, vitamins, fats, proteins and carbohydrates needed for good health. If, under the stressful conditions of capture, relocation and the adoption process, these horses are switched to a high-protein hay and fed only once or twice a day, problems such as scours (diarrhea), colic or other dietary upsets can develop.

In acordance with United States Department of Interior guidelines, a horse in good condition is described as follows: ribs cannot be visually distinguished but can easily be felt; backbone is not visible; hip bones do not show; withers are distinguished but do not protrude; shoulders and neck blend smoothly into body. Although this is a good general description, even in fit condition some older horses may have lightly visible ribs, and a genetically narrow horse may have a high backbone. Your veterinarian will help you in assessing your horse's condition.

When they are adopted, most wild horses are not in the type of top condition they will achieve with proper care. Each horse will have different nutritional needs depending on his size, age, condition and what kind and how much exercise or training he receives. Stress and even the weather will also affect dietary needs. Some wild horses that have long experienced poor diet, high-stress conditions or medical problems may take as long as a year to become physically fit. It will be your responsibility to bring your adopted horse to his highest potential through proper medical care, correct feeding and consistent caring. Your newly adopted wild horse will be totally dependent on you.

WATER

Often we don't think of water as a part of the horse's diet, but it is one of the most important nutrients. Not only does the horse need water to prevent dehydration, but water is needed for the production of saliva to aid in digestion, to move nutrients to the cells, remove waste and to regulate body heat. Without water a horse could die in two or three days. A horse may drink as little as five or six gallons a day during the winter, but during the summer he might consume as much as thirty gallons a day or more. Generally, an idle horse should drink his weight in water every two weeks. Water weighs about 8 pounds per gallon, which means that the average, 800-pound adult wild horse should drink a minimum of 7½ gallons per day. Factors such as heat, shelter, diet, age, condition, work, individual needs and stress will demand higher consumption.

Fresh water should be available to a horse at all times. The only exception is when a horse has been worked hard and is overheated. Until a heated horse is cool, offer water only in small sips. You can tell when a horse is cool by placing your hand on the area between the front legs. If the area does not feel damp or hot to the touch, it is generally safe to offer water.

Wild horses will not be familiar with the many types of automatic

A HORSE IN GOOD CONDITION. TWINKLES WITH LYN KAMER IN 1989 AFTER WINNING THE GRAND CHAMPIONSHIP IN THE JERSEY DEVIL 50, A 50-MILE ENDURANCE RIDE SPONSORED BY THE NEW JERSEY TRAIL RIDING ASSOCIATION.

water units and other containers used with domestic horses. If your stabling facilities have push-type or automatic water units, it is safest to provide your newly adopted wild horse with an alternate water source until you are sure he has learned to drink from these unfamiliar systems. (It is important that metal push-type water units are placed out of direct sunlight; otherwise the horse will burn his sensitive lips while trying to drink.)

During the winter in cold climates, you may need to use a tank heater to insure that your horse is consuming adequate water. A base temperature of 40 to 45 degrees F should be warm enough. In cold climates, rubber stock tanks, such as those made by Rubbermaid, appear to keep water slightly warmer in cold weather and cooler in hot weather.

It is important that water containers be cleaned on a regular basis to prevent the growth of harmful bacteria or other problems. A horse's water consumption can decrease to a dangerously low level if water is dirty, too hot, too cold or otherwise undrinkable.

SOME WILD HORSES HAVE EXPERIENCED A POOR DIET OVER A LONG PERIOD OF TIME.

SUPPLEMENTS

At the LIFE Equine Center, newly arrived horses are given ¼ to ½ teaspoon of Conklin's Fastrack Liquid Dispersible per day to help their digestive system. This should be mixed in a small enough water container that the horse consumes the entire amount in a single day. If the horse develops loose stools, cut back the amount of Fastrack. After the horse has begun to eat grain, you can substitute Fastrack Micro Feed powder, according to directions. The natural microorganisms in this product help your horse develop the proper gut functions needed for good digestion and metabolism of feed, which may have been diminished during the stress of roundup, transport and adoption.

SALT

Salt is an essential mineral in your horse's diet. In general a horse should be provided with at least 60 grams of salt per day. There are two basic ways of providing salt to your horse: salt blocks or loose granular salt. Salt may be purchased in three types: plain, iodized and trace mineral. Some horses have a decided preference for the type of salt and the way in which it is provided. Some horses will refuse one type of salt in block form but readily accept it in loose form. Ideally, a horse should have two types of salt available, one in block form and the other in a salt box containing the loose form.

Some states* are noted for having soil deficient in iodine. If you pasture your horse in or purchase hay from one of these areas, it may be advisable to provide your horse with iodized salt, in either block or loose form. As with any dietary question, you should discuss your horse's salt needs with your veterinarian.

Pacific Molasses offers a salt block called Sweet-Lix that provides minerals, vitamins and a fly-control ingredient to prevent the development of stable flies and houseflies in the manure of treated horses. Sweet-Lix seems to be readily accepted by most wild horses, although horses may consume more than necessary of the blocks at one time because of the high molasses content. A special salt block holder is available to prevent overconsumption.

FEED

Almost every horse owner and feed and supplement manufacturer will tell you that they have a magic formula that makes a horse

---

*California, Colorado, Illinois, Indiana, Iowa, Michigan, Montana, Nebraska, Nevada, New York, North Dakota, Ohio, Oregon, South Dakota, Utah, Washington and Wisconsin.

not only look better and run faster, but even act smarter. Although complicated formulas and high-priced supplements may be necessary for the horse that works hard, the owner of the average horse needs to use only simple guidelines and common sense in feeding a horse. If your newly adopted horse is free of parasites and is steadily gaining weight, and if his coat is shedding out to reveal shiny, healthy hair, you can generally feel comfortable that progress is being made.

It is advisable for first-time horse owners to purchase some type of unit to weigh feed. An inexpensive unit called Farm-n-Barn Scale is available from Valley Vet Supply in Marysville, Kansas. An ordinary baby scale can also be used.

Food for a horse is divided into two categories: roughages and concentrates. Roughages are feed such as hay and forage, or pasture. The bulk and fiber found in roughages are essential to your horse's health. Roughages are the basic component of your horse's diet. Some horses can be very healthy eating roughages alone.

Concentrates are feeds such as corn, oats, barley and bran. Concentrates can provide extra calories, higher protein and more fats and carbohydrates than some hays, but they provide very little fiber. Horses cannot be healthy on concentrates alone.

Hay

Hay is classified as one of two varieties: grass hay or legume hay. Both have advantages and disadvantages. As you will see in the partial list of hays listed below, the quality, nutrient and protein content and palatability vary depending on the type or variety, the location where it is grown and even the time it is cut.

Grass hay generally has a higher fiber content and a lower protein content than legume hay. The average grass hay has a protein content of 4 percent to 15 percent, while a legume hay such as alfalfa averages from 15 percent to 18 percent protein content. When the hay is cut affects not only the protein content but how the hay tastes to your horse. Generally, grass hays should be cut in pre-bloom or early-bloom stage. At this stage it is highest in protein, lowest in fiber and highest in palatability and digestibility. Alfalfa is usually cut when about 10 percent of the field is in bloom. After that the hay becomes coarser, with a lower protein and vitamin content.

Timothy hay is one of the most popular grass hays. The second and later cuttings, cut at prebloom or early bloom stage, have the highest palatability and quality, with a nutritional content of about 12.3 percent. The same hay cut at midbloom or late bloom will have a protein content of about 8.3 percent.

Coastal Bermuda grass hay is a popular grass hay in southern regions of the United States. It has a protein content similar to that of early-bloom timothy. As with timothy, second and later cuttings are usually recommended.

Bluestem grass hay, popular in Central Plains regions, is highly palatable. Bluestem has a protein content of about 5.4 percent.

Smooth bromegrass hay, grown usually in the Great Plains region, is accepted by most horses, though it is generally considered more palatable in a bromegrass-legume mix. The protein content of second-cutting, midbloom, smooth brome hay is about 11.8 percent. If the hay is allowed to mature before cutting, the protein content drops sharply to about 5.8 percent.

Wheat grass hay is most common in the Northern Plains, where it is cut early before it begins to bloom. Wheat grass becomes very tough and fibrous as it matures and loses its protein content. Prebloom wheat grass has a protein content of about 8.1 percent.

Sudan grass hay is grown throughout the United States. It should be cut at prebloom or early-bloom stage for greatest palatability and nutritional value. It contains about 9.7 percent protein. *Warning:* if cut too early, sudan grass may contain high amounts of prussic acid, which can be toxic.

Johnsongrass hay is grown in the southern regions. It should be cut at early bloom and has about a 7.6 protein content.

Orchard grass hay is grown in many areas throughout the United States. Although it is of fairly good quality when cut at the early-bloom stage, it becomes unpalatable and too low in nutrient content if cut later. Orchard grass cut early has an average protein content of 9.0 percent.

Cereal grass hays are made from grain crops, usually have a high nutrient value and are very palatable for horses when cut while still green. The most popular of the cereal hays are oat, barley and wheat. Second-cutting oat hay averages 9.2 percent protein content. Second-cutting barley has a protein content of about 8.7 percent. Second-cutting wheat has a protein content of about 7.5 percent.

Alfalfa is the most widely fed legume hay. Generally, alfalfa is higher in protein content, calcium and vitamin content than grass or cereal hays. Alfalfa may contain more protein than most mature nonworking horses need. If alfalfa is the main portion of your horse's diet, you may need to feed smaller amounts or reduce the use of concentrates. It is also easier for an inexperienced person to overfeed alfalfa. If you are a new horse owner, it may be advisable to feed an alfalfa-mix hay or grass hay. Early-bloom, second-cutting alfalfa has an average protein content of 18.4 percent. The same hay cut in midbloom has an average of 17.1 percent. Full bloom averages 15.9 percent, while mature bloom averages 13.6 percent protein content.

Whatever type you use, there are several points to look for in quality hay.

- Improperly harvested and cured hay may be dusty and cause respiratory problems. Watch for dust in newly opened bales.
- Hay should have a pleasant odor. Hay that smells musty or offensive may contain mold that can be fatal to your horse. Mold may show up as white patches, as black spots as you open the bale or as stripes on the outside of the bale.
- Hay should be free of weeds and other foreign material.
- Each type of hay has a normal color; for example, the inside of an alfalfa bale should be green. Fading or some discoloration from sun bleaching can be expected on the outside of the bale on hay stored outdoors.
- Hay stems should not be course or tough, and there should be plenty of leaves on the stem. Hay that is too mature when cut or that is damaged by weather or improperly dried will lose leaves and considerable nutritional value.
- Check grass and cereal hays such as barley for rough, sharp spikes, called awns or beards, on the seed. These can cause sores on the horse's mouth and lips or become embedded, creating ulcers in the mouth.

A pearl of wisdom from horsewoman Glenda Williams about hay that might be bad: "When in doubt, throw it out."

Hay cubes are most commonly made of alfalfa, but other hays are sometimes used. The cubes are produced in a variety of shapes but are most commonly 1¼″ by 1¼″ by 2″. Most companies guarantee a protein percentage of 16 percent for their product.

Hay cubes have several advantages to owners. They are easy to store in bulk or packaged, they can be measured easily, and they contain less dust than baled hay. In areas of high wind there is less loss. However, because of their rectangular shape, the cubes do not fit evenly into a measuring container, and as much as a pound can be lost to "air space." It is advisable to weigh each feeding when using cubes.

Many horses have lived their entire lives on cubes alone without any problems. The same general rules for selection of good hay apply to the selection of cubes.

Some concern has been expressed that horses are more prone to choke on cubes, but studies at the University of California have failed to confirm this. A valid concern is that greedy eaters may bolt the cubes. Reduced chewing and faster eating time reduces the amount of saliva that is mixed with the food, which can enter the digestive tract unprepared and cause impactions and colic. Greedy eaters can be slowed down by spreading cubes out in a large feeder or placing fist-size rocks in the feeder.

As with any change of diet, it is a good idea to introduce hay cubes gradually, say over a two-week period, and to watch your horse closely during the transition period. Also some horses may psychologically require more chewing time than cubes can provide. If your horse begins to develop a vice, such as chewing wood or other materials, one reason may be a need for additional chewing. Hay added to the diet may satisfy this need.

Pelleted feeds appear to be the wave of the future. With the high cost of producing hay, feed products that would not normally be consumed by horses can be incorporated into pellets, producing a highly palatable and nutritious feed. Pellets come in two basic varieties: hay only and complete, which contains hay, grain mixture, vitamins, minerals and salt.

Like hay cubes, pellets are easy to transport, store and feed. Older horses with poor teeth, foals, horses prone to colic, horses that travel overnight and horses with heaves are good candidates for pelleted feed. It is also advisable to feed 5 to 7 pounds of grass hay per day for bulk and fiber content.

Neither cube nor pelleted feeds should be used as the sole feed for wild horses until they are fit and adjusted to domestic life. They do make an excellent source of extra calories and protein and can be used as the third meal.

For the first few days, hay should be placed close to the corral wall to help prevent the horse from feeding and defecating in the same place. Remember, these animals are accustomed to eating on the ground and moving continually. Additionally, wild horses are reluctant to put their heads in any type of feeder that restricts their sight. Ground feeding may be necessary until your horse is comfortable with its surroundings.

Your horse should be weaned from ground feeding as soon as possible. When a horse eats hay from the ground, sand and other dirt particles are ingested along with feed. These particles can become impacted in the intestines and cause life-threatening medical problems. Sand colic combined with parasites is the number two killer of horses in the United States.

Concentrates

Among the many types of grain concentrates, the most common are oats and corn.

One of the most popular grains used by horse owners is oats, which has a higher fiber content than corn or barley and is considered a safer feed. Unfortunately, it is also more expensive. There is also a large variation in quality. Look for oats that are plump and full of starch, heavy and with a low proportion of husk to kernel, rather than thin and mostly fiber. Do not purchase oats that are dusty or that contain large amounts of weeds, seeds or other foreign material. If you have a question about the quality of oats, taste a few kernels yourself. There should be no sour or bitter taste. Because horses do not chew their food as much as they should, many of the whole oats are passed through their systems undigested. For this reason, it may be more economical to purchase higher-priced rolled or crimped oats rather than the lower-priced whole oats. Crimped or rolled oats improve digestibility by 5 to 7 percent. Foals and horses with poor teeth should always have crimped or rolled oats.

Corn, the second most popular grain fed to horses, is available in many types and forms. The color may range from white to yellow, either being a good feed, although yellow corn does have a higher vitamin A content. Corn is very high in calorie, or energy, content. The fact that it is high in fat with a low fiber content makes it more economical than feeding oats. Corn is available as whole, crushed, cracked or steamed. As with whole oats, some whole corn passes through the horse's system undigested. Young horses and older horses with dental problems should not be fed whole corn. With some corn that is crushed or ground (and with cracked corn that is too finely rolled), the small particles have an increased tendency to ferment rapidly in the digestive tract; when this hap-

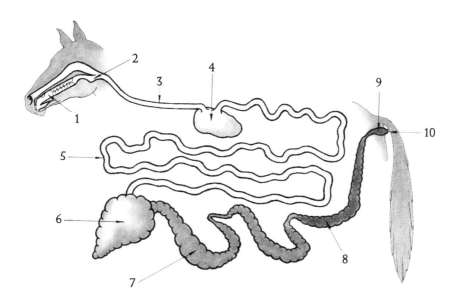

DIGESTIVE SYSTEM.
1. BUCCAL CAVITY
2. PHARYNX
3. OESOPHAGUS
4. STOMACH—APROX. 2½ GALS.
5. SMALL INTESTINE—APROX. 2¼ GALS.
6. CAECUM—APROX. 7¾ GALS.
7. LARGE COLON—APROX. 18½ GALS.
8. SMALL COLON—APROX. 5¼ GALS.
9. RECTUM
10. ANUS

pens, the possibility for colic increases. Cracked corn is rolled lightly with rollers that crack the outside of the kernel, allowing better penetration of saliva and easier mastication. Steamed flecked corn is the top of the line for feeding horses. Because this type of corn comes out of the flaking machine damp, it is important to check closely for musty odor or discoloration, such as bluish, grayish or greenish streaks, which indicate mold.

YOUR HORSE'S DIETARY NEEDS

There are several ways to determine a horse's dietary needs. The methods below have all been used successfully on wild horses. A horse that is thin, in poor health or rapidly growing will gain weight more efficiently if fed in numerous small feedings spaced evenly throughout the day. Usually three or four feedings are best. Ideally even a well horse will do best on three feedings per day. Two feedings per day is the minimum safe number. If the diet you choose does not divide into even feedings, provide the largest feeding in the evening. You will need to discuss with your veterinarian which diet he or she feels best suits your horse's needs.

Plan A

Total hay consumption per day should be determined by the weight of the horse when in good condition. *Example:* Your horse weighs 700 pounds and it should weigh 800 pounds. Feed would be calculated as 800 pounds divided by 100 = 8 × 2 pounds of oat, barley, grass, full-bloom or mature alfalfa or alfalfa-mix hay = 16 pounds of feed per day divided by three feedings = 5⅓ pounds of hay per feeding. This would be fed as 5 pounds in the morning, 5 pounds at noon and 6 pounds in the evening. Alfalfa hay would be figured at 800 pounds divided by 100 = 8 × 1.6 pounds of alfalfa hay = approximately 13 pounds of feed per day.

Nutrient Requirements of Growing Horses
900 lb. Mature Weight

Age in Months	Body weight	Calories
3	200	10,440
6	400	12,410
12	550	13,630
18	725	14,100
42	900	13,680

Composition of Common Hays

	Type	Approx. calories per lb.
Alfalfa		
	early bloom	1,057
	midbloom	1,021
	full bloom	953
	mature	880
Coastal Bermuda grass		
	overall average	880
Meadow Fescue		
	overall average	889
Oat		
	overall average	889
Orchard grass		
	overall average	839
Timothy		
	prebloom	1,061
	midbloom	880
	late bloom	862
Wheat		
	overall average	866

Composition of Common Grains

Type	Approx. calories per lb.
Barley	1,660
Corn	1,819
Oats	1,402

Plan B

Feed oat, barley, grass or alfalfa-mix hay, with a maximum of 3 percent of total body weight per day, until proper weight is obtained. To feed, you will have to know how much your horse weighs, be able to judge how much weight it needs to gain, and when he has reached that weight. A BLM wrangler or wild horse specialist at the adoption facility can give you a fairly accurate weight of your horse as he goes home and how much he needs to gain. Your veterinarian will be able to advise you when your horse has reached his proper body weight. *Example:* An 800-pound horse can be fed a maximum of 24 pounds per day. Your horse will gain an average of fifteen pounds per week on this diet. You should refigure the total body weight at the end of each week.

Plan C

This feeding program is based on calorie needs of the idle growing horse at various stages of growth. Although this diet is more precise, it also has a higher chance of dietary upset. Check with your veterinarian before starting this diet. The charts below will help you figure your horse's needs:

Example: You own a growing horse approximately eighteen months old; it weighs approximately 725 pounds and is being worked lightly. He will need approximately 14,100 calories per day. Feed would be calculated as 725 pounds divided by 100 = 7.25 × 2 pounds of oat, barley, grass, mature alfalfa or alfalfa-mix hay = 14.5 pounds of hay per day. Consult the Composition of Common Hays chart for the type of hay you are using. Using mature alfalfa, which has 880 calories per pound, you would multiply 14.5 × 880 calories per pound = 12,760 calories. Subtact this number from 14,100 calories needed per day = 1,240 calories still needed per day, which can come from added grains, concentrates or supplements.

Many wild horses are underweight at the time of adoption. Unfortunately putting weight on a horse is not just a matter of feeding more hay. Too much hay too fast can not only cause dietary upsets but leave your horse with an unattractive "hay belly." The LIFE Equine Center recommends using diet A for one week, then gradually introducing diet C over a two-week period. They recommend adding to this diet Borden's Bene Bac Lactobacillus Paste, Conklin's Fastrack Non-runiment Paste or Conklin's Fastrack Liquid Dispersible in the water, according to directions.

For horses under two years, especially those who are underweight or may have been deprived of calcium, an excellent supplement is Borden's EN-PRO, used alone or in addition to grain, depending on your horse's need.

As with any diet questions, it is important that you work with your veterinarian to determine what is best for your horse. Remember, there is no such thing as a dumb question, and it is better to be safe than sorry.

.7.

AT THE ADOPTION CENTER

There are a few things that new wild horse owners need to take to the adoption center:

A sturdy halter. A double-stitched, nylon-webbing halter, two or three layers thick, is a good choice. Do not use a snap-under-the-throatlatch type of halter unless you are purchasing an adjustable halter for an orphan or weanling foal. Do not use a rope halter.

A long cotton rope, ¾ inch to 1 inch thick and about 25 feet long. Cotton rope may not last as long as nylon rope, but it is easier on the horse and there is less chance of rope burns. This rope is left on the horse and is called a dragline. The rope will drag on the ground behind the horse, allowing you to pick it up from a safe distance during the first few weeks after adoption.

Although you could put a snap on the dragline to attach it to the halter, the snap hitting the horse's chin as he moves may startle or injure the horse. The wranglers at the adoption facility will be happy to tie the dragline to the halter. Use a heavy tape, such as electrical tape, around the end of the dragline to prevent it from unraveling; a knot on the end of the rope could catch on the corral or stall and cause injury to the horse. At home, as the horse moves he will step on the dragline and learn to respect restraint. Most draglines last only two to four weeks because they become cut and worn as the horse moves about and steps on them.

If possible, bring someone who has had experience with wild horses, or at least an experienced horseperson who admires wild horses. He or she will be able to look at the good and poor points of the horses you are interested in, without all the emotions that will be racing around inside you.

A copy of this book. While you look over the horses, refer to the charts at the end of this chapter regarding conformation of the horse's body.

Your wallet! Adoption fees are $125.00 for horses and $75.00 for burros. The BLM will accept cash, a money order or a certified check only.

Do not bring treats like carrots, apples, sugar or cookies. Wild horses won't know what they are—treats are an acquired taste.

TRAILERS

A stock-type trailer with the center partition taken out works the best with most horses. A regular two-horse trailer is okay if it's a step-in type with a completely closed-in back. If your trailer has "butt straps," do not allow them to be fastened when the horse is loaded. Trailers with drop-ramp tailgates are not allowed by the BLM, for safety reasons.

Hay nets in the trailer are not a good idea. If they are hung high, the movement can startle the horse; if they are hung low, the horse may get a hoof caught. Tape an "x" shape across the windows.

ADOPTION DAY IS ALMOST HERE.

If your travel time to get home will be more than 24 hours, the BLM requires that the horse be taken off the trailer to a secure corral for hay and water and to rest for at least five hours. Make arrangements ahead of time.

If you are planning to adopt more than one horse, a stock trailer is preferable because of the larger space inside. Wild horses are accustomed to being shipped with other horses. The BLM may require you to have partitions to separate the horses, so it is best to check. Needless to say, it's better not to ship a stallion and a mare together.

If you are using a trailer that has a center partition, try to use one where the partition goes all the way to the floor. It is easy for a horse to panic and slide under a partial partition.

Recheck your plans on how you will back the trailer up to the corral and unload the horse when you get home. Remember, your horse will not know how to walk on a lead.

Before leaving home, look over your equipment. Check your corral or stall, your feeding and water buckets, feed, halter, dragline, and other necessities.

EVALUATING THE HORSES

When you arrive at the corrals, you will notice that each horse has a numbered tab tied around its neck. Each horse has a separate identification number. In some states the color of the tag will tell you if the horse is a mare, gelding or stallion. Each horse will also have a freeze brand, which tells the government agency the horse's birth year and individual registration number. On dark horses this shows up as a white marking on the left side of the neck. On light-colored horses the brand shows up dark.

Freeze branding is a painless process using liquid nitrogen. The brand is used to permanently identify the horse as a BLM wild horse or burro. A key explaining the symbols of the brand is included in the BLM booklet, "So You'd Like to Adopt a Wild Horse or Burro?"

As you are looking over the horses, write down the numbers on the tags of the ones that stay close to the fence when you are there or, better yet, those who poke their noses through the fence to say hi to you. These horses are curious about people and will be easier to gentle. This may be one of the priorities on your list, especially if you are unfamiliar with horses and training. The horses that won't come near or that dash away from you are more independent or may be more nervous.

Physical Characteristics

Go over in your mind all the different points you are interested in: size, age, color and gender. Once you have picked out a few horses that come close to your ideals, tell the man or woman who works at the center. They will go into the pen and have individual horses move around for you. Watch carefully how the horse moves. This is extremely important. Try to detect any signs of lameness and to gauge the horse's usefulness for the function you want him to fulfill. Evaluating the horse's movements is also im-

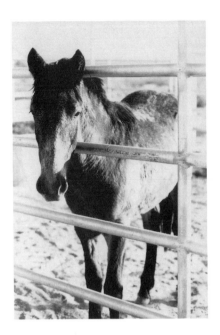

A CURIOUS HORSE MAY BE EASIER TO GENTLE.

portant for determining riding comfort, as anyone knows who has been bounced like a rubber ball while riding a choppy-gaited horse.

Look at conformation, too—how the horse is built or put together. The illustrations of conformation faults (see pages 88–89) will help guide you. Use your imagination and look beyond a rough or long winter coat, patches of mud, unkempt mane and tail and even some lack of weight and muscle tone. Luckily, wild horses seldom have leg or feet problems. Because of their slow growth and high bone density, wild horses develop sound legs and strong hooves that can stand up to the rough terrain that they have lived in.

Your friend with knowledge about horses will be invaluable now in giving you the benefit of an experienced eye and cool logic. But if he or she is used to prime horses in top shape, the sight of the wild horses at the adoption facility may be dismaying. We promise you that with good care and a little time these horses will be as sleek and handsome as their domestic cousins.

WITH TIME AND GOOD CARE, WILD HORSES WILL BE AS SLEEK AND HANDSOME AS DOMESTIC HORSES. RENO, A FEW MONTHS AFTER ADOPTION.

Personality

How does a prospective horse deal with others? Is he the bossy type, an easygoing Mr. Nice Guy or the shy, shrinking violet type?

Here are some ways to judge a horse's personality:

The bold dominant horse will be leading the charge when the herd runs. He will be the first to drink the water or go to the hay trough. This horse may spend a lot of time pinning his ears back and chasing or herding the others around.

The easygoing horse will be running with the herd but will have the confidence to leave the herd sometimes and scout around on his own. He is not so quick to dash away from you, and he doesn't react violently to every little noise.

The shy horse will run from the other horses' threats. He will yield his place at the trough to a stronger horse. He may peek around other horses from a safe distance or try to stay in the center of the band.

If the horse had his ears back almost all the time, he's either the Big Boss, is in pain or has a sour-pickle personality. Often this type of horse will be difficult to gentle.

Possible Illness

Most horses will stay close to other horses, so a horse that's always by itself may be ill. A horse who isn't feeling up to par will appear listless or dull. Look for any discharge from the nose or eyes, and listen for coughing.

Wild horses often develop respiratory problems from the stress of capture, captivity, transport and dietary change. Be alert to these symptoms.

Behavior

When you have narrowed the choice down to a few candidates, ask a person working at the center what he or she knows about the horse. Ask questions like: "How does this horse behave with other horses? What have you observed about this horse? How big do you think he will get? How long since the horse has been captured? How many adoption facilities has he been in?" Ask whatever comes to mind, even questions about wild horses you may have written down beforehand. People at the adoption center welcome questions, because they sincerely want the horses to go to suitable, happy homes where they'll have good care. Although BLM personnel at satellite adoptions may not have as much information about the horse as those at permanent adoption facilities, they should be able to give you some information.

Before you make up your mind, there is one more thing to consider. Look inside yourself this time, instead of at the horses. Make sure the horse really appeals to you, that you have a decided feeling that it is this horse that you want to dedicate hundreds of hours and months of your time to. You will be spending a lot of time together, so this is almost like picking a marriage partner. Let your emotions go, then deliberately calm yourself down and think clearly. Is this the best horse for you or for your family? Be honest— you don't want to have a short honeymoon.

You have talked it over with the people at the center, family members and your knowledgeable horse friend. You have battled the tug-of-war within you: the bay or chestnut, the black mare or the buckskin gelding . . . and finally made the decision: "That one— that will be my new wild horse."

If you weren't required to do so before you selected your horse, you should now go to the office to fill out the paperwork. With your adoption papers, you will receive information about the horse: its age, sex, when and where it was rounded up, and its medical records, including information on its worming, inoculations and tests for diseases.

Presently the moment of truth comes: parting with the precious greenbacks in your wallet. Get used to kissing them good-bye. Horses have a dandy way of separating you from your paycheck.

SATELLITE ADOPTIONS

The procedure may differ slightly at the various centers. In addition to the regular BLM adoption offices, temporary satellite adoption sites are set up throughout the year for people located far from the permanent centers.

The satellite adoptions are held over a period of two or three days, usually on a weekend, with a few truckloads of wild horses and sometimes burros brought in to a facility such as a stockyard, fairground or college campus. Some BLM offices send reminder notices about the adoption to approved applicants, but others do not.

Not all satellite adoptions have the same procedures, so it is a good idea to find out before you go what will be expected of you and what the schedule will be. At some satellites there will be a meeting for all adopters to explain the rules of adopting a wild horse or burro, and you will be assigned a number.

Those who fill out their applications and are approved will have first choice. At other satellites your number will be put into a hat; as your number is called, you are allowed to choose your horse. People who stop by and decide to adopt will have a chance once all the prior applicants have chosen their favorites.

Final title for ownership of the horse may be applied for after you have taken good care of the horse for one year. The BLM office in your district may send you a title application twelve months after the adoption. If they do not, contact the BLM for instructions. You must send back the title application signed by a veterinarian, humane officer or someone authorized at the BLM.

For a listing of satellite dates and locations, call or write the closest Adopt-A-Horse office. See Appendix 1.

TAKING YOUR HORSE HOME

Once the adoption papers are signed, your new horse will be run down the alleyway and into the loading chute. This will be a nervous time for your new horse, so stand back from the chute. Do not try to touch the horse through the chute. A fast movement by your horse could result in your arm being pinned between the horse and bars, with a resulting broken bone or worse. Don't be shy about asking other people to stand back, too. The wranglers will ask you if they want any help.

Your halter and dragline will be put on your horse by the BLM wranglers. This could be quick or it may take some time, depending on the horse's cooperation. The new sounds and smells at the adoption site and the close confinement of the chute may panic some horses. If your horse is one of those that rears and causes a fuss in the chute, don't think you've picked a killer horse! It is certainly within the normal range of behavior for a wild, untrained horse to act up in the chute. The horse is separated from the security of the herd, and he's going to be upset. Most of the time a horse that acts up is sensitive or frightened.

When the halter and dragline are on, the horse will be sent down the chute into the trailer. It may sound like a hurricane's coming— Whoosh! Once the horse is inside, the wranglers will close the trailer door before your hurricane blows out of there again.

Give your wild-eyed friend a moment to settle down before you pull the trailer away. When you do start to move, accelerate slowly

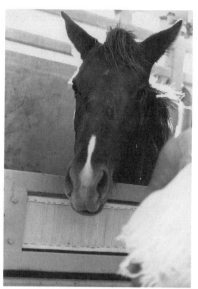

THE LOADING CHUTE IS A FRIGHT-
ENING PLACE FOR YOUR HORSE.

WHEN IT'S TIME FOR THE HORSE TO
BE LOADED, THE TRAILER IS BACKED
UP TO THE CHUTE.

and smoothly. When you are driving slowly in a straight line but before you pull onto the main road, it is a good idea to apply the brakes and stop the truck completely. You may hear some bumping around from the trailer, but this is a message to the horse that he needs to balance himself and set his feet for the ride ahead.

The majority of wild horses are good travelers, having been shipped many miles between capture sites and adoption centers.

As you are driving home, you may want to review your plan for backing up the trailer to the corral.

TAKING THE HORSE OUT OF THE TRAILER

You're home at last, and you are bound to feel tired. Before you take the horse out of the trailer, pause a moment to relax and have an energy snack.

While you are relaxing, think about the big P word—patience. This means you are not in a hurry. The horse is still frightened; if possible, he shouldn't have a scary experience right away at his new home. The horse needs reassurance and soft words, not angry shouts like, "Get out of the trailer, stupid!"

Once you have backed the trailer up to the corral, make sure there are no gaps that the horse can get through. If your horse has been tied in the trailer, untie his head first. Allow the horse to settle down and then open the trailer door. If the horse panics when you open the door and he is tied up, he may slip under the partition, turn his body or cause some other "wreck," so please untie the head first.

It is better not to have a lot of people standing around the trailer or corral gate, because this may make the horse want to stay inside. Even without a gang of well-wishers standing there, sometimes the horse feels safer in the trailer and refuses to come out. Let it relax, then walk alongside the trailer to see if your movement will help the horse get going. No loud noises or claps, though, which might startle the horse and have him scramble around and get hurt.

If you have the time, leave the gate open and stay away from the trailer for a while. The horse should get bored and come out on his own.

Occasionally a horse will need more persuasion or you may need to get the horse out quickly because of oncoming darkness or other reasons. Walk to the front of the trailer and make a few clucking sounds to see if this will encourage the horse to move away from you and out of the trailer. Try this several times with clucking or other sounds. Even a light tap on the trailer wall may encourage the horse to move away and out. If it does not and it is important to move the horse out of the trailer, you may want to try a more aggressive method: using a broom or a rod with a small flag attached to the end, walk to the side of the trailer that the horse is standing on, then calmly insert the broom through an opening, tapping the horse on the shoulder closest to you while again making the clucking sound. This should encourage the horse to turn and move away from you. As the horse turns, continue to tap along the shoulder toward the rear until the horse is facing the opening. Now lightly tap the horse's rear end, encouraging him to move forward and out of the opening. Attempt this several times. If the horse becomes panicked, stop, allow the horse to calm down and then proceed again.

If your horse is in a two-horse trailer, you will need to back the horse out without turning it around. Again use the least aggressive method first. Occasionally a horse will need more persuasion. Slowly untie the lead rope, if needed, allow the horse to settle down and then open the trailer door. Just your standing at the horse's head may encourage him to back away from you. If not, slowly insert the broom in front of the horse, causing him to back out of the trailer.

IN THE CORRAL

When the horse is out of the trailer, quickly but quietly close the corral gate *before* pulling the trailer away. If you have had problems and the horse has gotten away, refer to chapter 12, "A New Freedom," which includes methods for catching wild horse escapees.

In the corral, the horse may be bothered by the dragline hitting against his hind legs or by stepping on it. Keep in mind that to a horse any unnatural object touching his legs or hooves is frightening. Your horse will become used to this, and the dragline will act as the beginning of your training. Don't interfere unless the horse has gotten itself into serious trouble, such as being tangled up or caught on something. If that happens, move very carefully and slowly. The horse could struggle and you or the horse might be injured. It might be better to cut the dragline than to attempt to untangle it.

After the horse has settled down, enter the corral in a confident manner, with an attitude of "no big deal." When you come into the corral, the horse may roll his eyes or rush to the other side of the corral. Don't be concerned; just ignore the horse and proceed to check the water container and maybe spread some hay around.

It is rare that a wild horse will act in an aggressive manner or present you with a threatening attitude. If you feel that this is happening, exit the corral quickly while facing the horse. Methods of handling aggressive horses—usually cases in which horses have been mishandled by previous adopters or trainers—will be dealt with in later chapters.

The horse has had a lot of stress and excitement for one day. It's better not to try and work with the horse now. Leave him alone to get used to the sounds and smells of his new surroundings and any other horses that may live there.

INTO THE BARNSTALL

If your horse is going into a barnstall, you will handle the situation a little differently. As with a corral, back the trailer directly to the entrance of the barnstall or paddock (no larger than 24' by 24') attached to it. Proceed as described above, until your horse is in the barnstall or paddock.

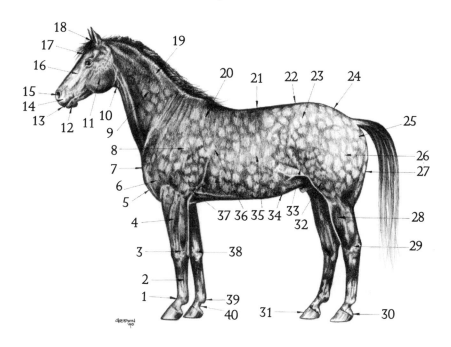

POINTS OF THE HORSE.

1.	FETLOCK JOINT	21.	BACK
2.	CANNON	22.	LOIN
3.	KNEE	23.	POINT OF HIP
4.	FOREARM	24.	CROUP
5.	CHEST	25.	BUTTOCK
6.	ARM	26.	THIGH
7.	POINT OF SHOULDER	27.	QUARTER
8.	SHOULDER	28.	GASKIN
9.	NECK	29.	HOCK
10.	THROATLATCH	30.	CORONET
11.	CHEEK	31.	HOOF
12.	LOWER LIP	32.	STIFLE
13.	UPPER LIP	33.	FLANK
14.	MUZZLE	34.	ABDOMEN
15.	NOSTRIL	35.	BARREL
16.	FACE	36.	HEART GIRTH
17.	FOREHEAD	37.	ELBOW
18.	POLL	38.	CHESTNUT
19.	CREST	39.	ERGOT
20.	WITHERS	40.	PASTERN

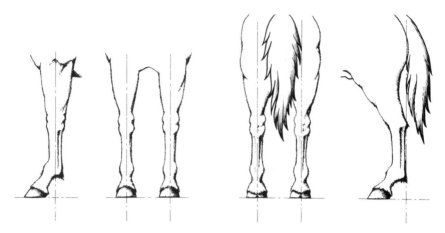

PROPER ALIGNMENT OF LEGS.

If you must take the horse down the center of the barn or
through an alleyway to get to the stall, take special precautions.
Have a regular household broom handy. Close off all the stall doors,
top and bottom, except your horse's, and block off any detours
with at least a 5½ foot solid barricade. Bales of hay will work nicely
to detour the horse. Remember to block off the area directly behind your horse's stall door. Make certain that once the horse is
off the trailer, the only route he can take is to the stall. After you
open the trailer, the horse may walk calmly off or he may come
flying. Be ready for both and all possibilities.

Warning: there is a false and dangerous idea that you can always
turn a horse by stepping in front of him and waving your hands.
Wrong! If a horse is panicked, he may not even be aware that he
is knocking you down as he runs you over. This method can be
used, but always allow yourself room to get out of the way.

If the barn has cement floors, the noise and feel of it could cause
the horse to become nervous and act as though he is walking on
eggs. If the horse keeps hesitating, encourage him with your voice
from behind. Walking in back of the horse, far out of kicking range,
will usually help him to keep moving forward. If the horse stops,
he may take that opportunity to think that he wants to go back to
the trailer. You could find yourself with a horse that is racing past
you up and down the alleyway, not only exciting the other horses

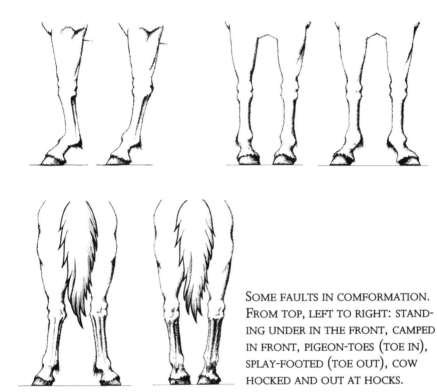

SOME FAULTS IN COMFORMATION. FROM TOP, LEFT TO RIGHT: STANDING UNDER IN THE FRONT, CAMPED IN FRONT, PIGEON-TOES (TOE IN), SPLAY-FOOTED (TOE OUT), COW HOCKED AND OUT AT HOCKS.

but endangering himself and you. If the horse stops and does not move forward when you make clucking noises, short whistles or other sounds, create a barrier with the broom to discourage the horse from going back toward the trailer. Continue to move forward with the barrier. Once the horse goes into the stall, gently shut the door. Don't slam it and send the horse to the rafters! The horse may run around the stall—the confinement or the dragline may be part of the reason, but he should soon calm down.

When the horse has settled, then you can quietly go in to check the water and hay. Inspect the stall one more time to make sure there are no sharp objects, nails or other objects that may be protruding and harm the horse.

In most cases, wild horses accept their new homes quickly, as long as they are treated with common sense and patience.

.8.

DAY ONE

Your newly adopted horse has received the luck of the draw: finding an owner who will care for and help him adjust to a new home and way of life. However, your horse doesn't know about his luck yet and is probably feeling very scared, lonely and vulnerable. Don't add any more stress or confusion to his already overloaded senses by doing too much too soon.

On the first day together, you simply want to let the horse settle in and get used to you. Your horse will show or "cue" you about how much you can accomplish. There are no set rules in gentling a wild horse, because each horse is different. A rare horse may allow you to approach and touch him the first day. Another may require weeks of slow, patient work even to be comfortable with you in the corral.

Horses have excellent memories, and first contacts with people are long remembered. Be sure that the horse's first impression of you is a relaxed and friendly one. As with a child, the horse's character is molded by how he is handled in the beginning. The nature of his early handling will affect his whole outlook and whether he sees man as friend or foe.

Adding a new horse to your family is very exciting. The first day home you'd probably like to have all your friends over to see him, but it's better to wait a week or two, for your horse's sake. Meeting a whole parade of faces, voices and smells would be upsetting to your horse. Consider these first days together as a time to learn about each other one on one, like a honeymoon with your horse! For your safety, until he is gentled you will want to have a friend or family member standing by while you work with your newly adopted horse.

As with all nervous newlyweds, you may feel strange and awkward around each other at first, but that will pass. Don't let that feeling shake your confidence that you can become friends and partners.

Men and women have been gentling and training horses for more than 5,000 years, so you can, too. The ways of gentling horses haven't changed that much over the centuries. The way is found through understanding several time-tested concepts:

Be patient. Remaining as calm as possible in all situations works best in winning the horse's trust and respect. Sometimes you will

THE WAYS OF GENTLING HORSES PROBABLY HAVEN'T CHANGED MUCH IN THE CENTURIES SINCE MONGOLIAN HORSEMEN TRAVELED THE PLAINS OF ASIA.

need to repeat things, and you will have to do so without getting angry or impatient.

Be quiet. Horses have extremely sharp hearing and respond best if you use soft, soothing sounds when you're around them. Loud, harsh sounds will excite the horse and also cause confusion, making learning and communication more difficult. To get the horse's attention, whistles, squeaks, clucking and kissing sounds are more effective than loud, abrupt noises.

Use body language. Besides using your voice to communicate with your horse, how you move your body—whether it is relaxed, confident or tense—will also send messages. How you smell is important to the horse too. For now, avoid powerful perfumes, aftershaves or hair sprays so the horse can smell the real you!

Make the right thing easy to do, and the wrong thing difficult or uncomfortable to do. The horse will soon realize that it works to his advantage to cooperate with people. He'll learn it's easier to put up with a human nearby while eating dinner than to keep running away and have an empty belly!

Move slowly. In the beginning, sudden movements will panic the horse. If your horse has his head deep in a feed trough, don't bounce up and say hi! From a distance, make a sound that lets the horse know you are coming.

Be consistent. Use the same signals and words for the same requests, *every time.*

Be kind. Horses are very intelligent, and enjoy affection and considerate handling.

Be confident. Your horse will follow the signals you are sending him. Don't assume there is going to be a problem! If you appear anxious and expect trouble, you'll probably get it.

Be calm. What isn't done today can be done tomorrow. If you run into a problem, ask yourself why the horse is reacting this way, then figure out what you can do to change his need to do that thing.

Enjoy your horse! Training a wild horse shouldn't become a contest to see how fast you can break your horse. If you can only be with your horse an hour a day, the world isn't going to fall apart. Just do what you can. Since each horse and each owner are unique, there can't possibly be any one method that's perfect for everyone. If something doesn't feel comfortable to you, find a new way to accomplish the same thing. Your attitude will be a major factor in how your horse responds to you and what kind of horse you end up with. If you believe training a horse is a battle of wills—as "I'll show this stupid horse who's boss!"—then it will be a battle, one in which everyone loses. You are teaching your horse so you can form a partnerhip, not forcing your control on the horse or trying to break his will.

You will notice that in some of the accompanying photographs the owner does not have a dragline on the horse. This is a matter of personal preference; lessons will be the same with or without the rope. For adopters who do not have experience with a lariat or lack the advantage of chutes or other restraining facilities, it is best to work with a dragline on the horse.

APPROACHING THE HORSE

When you first approach the horse, take a few minutes to check the corral. Is it secure? Are all the railings and posts in good condition? If so, take a few more minutes to observe the horse. Is he watching you? If not, make a low, comforting noise such as a kissing sound or a soft whistle. When the horse notices you, you can start coming closer to the corral.

A newly caught horse has a potentially strong flight reaction. He will watch to see exactly what you are doing. Many experienced horse trainers believe wild horses are easier to train than unhandled domestic horses, because wild horses give you their undivided attention.

One of the first things you should do is to judge your horse's flight distance. Observe how close you can come before the horse begins to panic; this is called flight distance. When you enter into a wild horse's flight space, the horse will feel threatened or alarmed, and his instinct is to flee. How far he runs will depend on how serious the threat is.

Wild horses have been observed continuing to graze with coyotes lying just a few yards away. If the coyotes stand up or display threatening behavior, the horses run, but only for a short distance. Then they stop and look to see if the danger has passed or if they should keep running. A wild animal never wastes energy unless it's absolutely necessary.

When the horse appears to accept your presence, it's time to enter the corral. While this may take several weeks with some horses, it is mentioned here because a surprising number of wild horses can be approached during the first few days.

You have established your right to share the horse's territory by being near or entering the corral when you are feeding or watering the horse. Walk in a confident manner. At the point when your horse begins to panic, enter just inside that distance.

Stand quietly and in a nonthreatening way, such as with your hands behind your back. If the horse shows extreme excitability, stop and act as though you had planned to only go this far. Don't react to the horse's excitement. In fact, a little laughter can help relieve the tension.

If you have the time, bring a chair, sit down *outside the corral*, read a book out loud, play a guitar, or just talk to your horse. It doesn't matter what you say. We do not recommend sitting inside the corral because if you have to move quickly the chair may hamper your movement. Family members can take turns visiting the horse. If you don't have time for a long, sit-down visit, try to make as many trips to the corral as possible, just to say hello.

As your horse becomes used to you at this distance, start coming closer until he appears to accept your presence, points his ears in your direction or greets you by turning around and looking at you.

Soon the horse will remain fairly calm when you are near. Watch the horse's ears. Are they aimed in your direction, listening to you? Horses have a high degree of curiosity, which will work to your advantage.

Each time your horse accepts you within his flight distance, advance a little closer, stopping when necessary, until you are inside the corral. An experienced horseperson may wish to start this process inside the corral, but those less familiar with horses should begin outside the corral, as explained above. You need to feel comfortable with the horse, so that the horse will read your confident body language and can begin to feel secure with you. If you have rounded off the corral corners, the horse will have no choice but to run in a circle as you enter the corral. When the horse starts to run away, walk calmly to the center of the corral. Soon the horse will realize that no matter how fast it runs, you are still the same distance away and are not trying to hurt him.

The horse will soon stop wasting energy and pause to look at you, perhaps aiming his ears in your direction to see how serious a threat you are. Spend a few minutes talking to the horse. Then point one arm toward the horse's rear end, to symbolically block off his escape, and point with the other arm the direction you want the horse to go.

The horse will start moving around and around the corral. This soon becomes tiring and frustrating to him because he's not getting anywhere.

"WATCH ME"

At this point, the horse is ready for a new lesson. The next time the horse attempts to slow down or stop, allow him to do so by stepping back, increasing the horse's territorial space. When the horse stops, give the command "Watch me." Of course, the horse does not understand the command word yet, but he may turn around to see what you are doing and reassess your "threat" status.

If the horse turns to face you, there is communication going on! Spend some time talking to the horse, but do not move forward unless the horse starts to move away.

If the horse does not look at you or starts to move away, step forward toward the rear end to move him around the corral again. The horse is doing what he wants (escaping from you) *and* what you want—moving forward. In reality, the horse is working with you for the first time.

When the horse slows down, take a step forward toward the rear end, to ask him to keep moving ahead. Do this several times, so that the horse is "giving" to your signals. The next time the horse slows down, retreat by stepping back and again attempt to

Point one arm; block off the horse's escape in that direction.

Point the other arm in the direction you want the horse to go.

IF THE HORSE DOES NOT LOOK AT YOU, STEP FORWARD TO MOVE IT
AROUND THE CORRAL AGAIN.

communicate by saying "Watch me." If the horse turns to face you,
you are getting through to the horse.

Continue this lesson until the horse decides it is more pleasant
to stand quietly and watch you than to run away. Remember not
to move toward the horse when he stops. Simply spend a few
minutes talking, or you could try blowing, which is what a horse
does.

NOSE CONTACT AND OTHER BODY LANGUAGE

A horse will approach a strange horse, animal, object, or human
by blowing in and out of his nostrils. This is not just an attempt
by the horse to identify the smell; it is a form of communication.

You can introduce yourself in a similar manner: blow through your nose or gently through your mouth. Your horse may step back, quite startled by your strange human smell, but will likely offer his nose to you again. You may start this introduction from as far away as 12 feet or more. As we might recognize an alien waving a foot in greeting, most horses appear to recognize your attempt as harmless and friendly. If you were a horse, questions such as your standing in the pecking order, sex and other personal data would all be answered in this simple greeting.

Your horse may offer to blow or snort back at you. Although most wild horses are not aggressive, a snort may be a sign of surprise at your unusual smell, or it may be a warning that you are coming too close.

Read the other body signals the horse is sending you. Are the ears lying back or pointed toward you? Is the horse curious about you, or telling you not to step any nearer? If you feel the horse is showing aggression, move him forward and away from you as described earlier.

If you have not rounded the corners of the corral, the horse will probably face the corner with his head in a lowered position. If the horse is frantically trying to find an escape route or challenging the fence, you are pushing too hard. Lessen the psychological pressure on the horse by backing up a few steps, a little toward the opposite direction you want the horse to travel. Each time the horse hesitates or slows down at a corner, step forward, pointing at his hind end, causing the horse to move ahead. Most likely there will be a specific corner where the horse wants to slow down. Anticipate this by more aggressively moving forward as he approaches that corner. Continue as described with the round corral above.

Eventually when the horse slows down you can step back and say "Watch me" and the horse will stay in that position while you talk to him. Then you can slowly hold out a hand and move closer to the horse. As the horse builds his trust in you, he will allow you to come closer each time.

Observe your horse carefully, so you'll know at what point to let up. Remember, advance until the horse becomes uncomfortable; then stop or retreat to the point where the horse is comfortable and relaxed again. Spend time talking to the horse,

SLOWLY HOLD OUT A HAND AND MOVE CLOSER TO THE HORSE.

AS THE HORSE BUILDS ITS TRUST IN YOU, IT WILL ALLOW YOU TO COME
CLOSER EACH TIME.

repeating the command "Watch me" at this distance. Then advance again. An advance may be only one step forward or many steps.

After the horse is doing it correctly, repeat this lesson for ten to fifteen minutes with the horse responding to your stepping back and giving the command "Watch me."

Actually touching the horse is dealt with in the following chapter. Right now, you are just concerned with letting the horse get used to you.

Feeding the newly adopted horse is a training lesson as well. If you bring hay into the corral and stand about 5 feet away for a few minutes, the horse has two choices: to go ahead and eat with you standing there, or to wait until you leave, even though he wants the hay now.

This doesn't have to be a battle of patience. Stay for five or ten minutes, then leave. This gives the horse a chance to relax and let his guard down. Come back later and try again until your horse is comfortable with you being at a close distance. Don't challenge the horse by staring at him.

If you divide the daily feed into many smaller feedings, standing nearby each time, the horse will soon accept your presence. When you come into the corral, the horse will probably get upset again, but he should settle down faster each time, as you remain calm and ignore any panic he displays.

Wild horses that have been in captivity for long periods of time or that have been adopted and returned to the BLM have often lost much of the flight reaction when they see a human. At this point they see a person as a semi-threatening being, but they have never bonded or developed a trusting relationship. Many wild horses will accept an adopter standing close or even touching them if they are not forced to look eye to eye or if the adopter is not standing within the horse's blind spot in front of his face.

THE INSTINCT TO FOLLOW

In 1989, Robin Rivello adopted a five-year-old mare she named Reno. Reno had been through several adoption facilities over the course of two years. At one center, she had injured herself trying to jump a 7-foot fence.

Robin said, "In the beginning, Reno was extremely wary. She had to overcome two years of not being too thrilled with people."

On the first day after adoption, she sat near Reno for more than three hours. "Reno wouldn't come near me," she said, "unless I turned my back on her, and then she'd come and gently nibble at my hair. If I turned, she'd move away."

In this type of situation, if you take a single step forward away from the horse with your back turned, the horse will probably follow you. It is a horse's natural behavior to follow. All you're doing is transferring the need to follow another horse to following a human.

When the horse comes behind you, say "Walk." The horse will have no idea what this means, but he will soon understand with repetition. If you continue for ten or fifteen minutes to give the "Walk" command and then stopping after a few steps, the horse might actually follow you as if he were on a lead line.

As the horse responds, you could hold out the hand nearest to him slightly, as if you are holding a lead line, or even slowly raise your hand to allow the horse to smell it. As the horse becomes comfortable with you, he will probably start to greet you face to face instead of from the back!

During the first few weeks, Robin spent many hours patiently sitting with Reno, talking quietly and offering handfuls of hay and grain. Finally, on the twelfth day after adoption Reno allowed herself to be touched.

Former racehorse trainer Lyn Kamer adopted two wild horses, Twinkles and Oregon's Little Star. She found that the more time you spend with them in the beginning, the better.

She remarked, "Both horses had at least five hours spent with them the first full day they were home, and two or three hours every day after that for weeks. Star had five to six hours spent with her every day for the first full week, and it really made a difference. She came as far in a week as Twinkles did in three weeks." This amount of time may not be possible for everyone, but spend as much time as you can. If you walk out to the corral ten times a day and just say hello, your horse will realize that you mean no harm and stop running away (wasting energy) every time you approach. It is too stressful to stay tense and suspicious, especially when the "threat" isn't doing anything scary.

BUILDING TRUST

Iris Fitzpatrick, an endurance rider with many years' experience with horses, adopted a five-year-old mare she named Idaho Roxie. Roxie had been through three adoption centers and had been in captivity for about a year.

Iris said it took several weeks to gain Roxie's trust, but after that she came along very quickly. Roxie was going well under saddle only three months after adoption.

Quick results may come with some horses, but don't get discouraged if yours isn't one of them. The main goal in the beginning is to establish a relationship of trust and friendship with your horse. This is not a competition to see how fast you can train your horse.

The majority of adopters find that once they develop a bond with their wild horse, further training is accomplished rapidly and with few problems. Most adopters agree that their wild horse is the smartest horse they ever handled.

Wild horse adopter Loretta Pambianchi said that her wild horse Ranger Bae picks up things so quickly that "I swear he was already trained and then turned out on the range!" Knowing and understanding the horse's personality helps in planning the approach to take in developing his potential. Shy, sensitive horses need to be handled quietly and carefully. Bold horses need a firmer approach that doesn't tolerate aggressive behavior. Easygoing horses work best with a moderate, mixed approach.

In the beginning, you will be learning how your horse reacts to things and the signs he uses to communicate. Everything the horse does can tell you something about how he is feeling. The accompanying chart of common horse body language signals should help you understand what your horse is saying to you.

Generally, wild horses have few bad habits such as rearing, striking or kicking, unless they have been cornered or bullied. These habits usually come from association with humans.

Horse signals and body language chart.

EARS

1. HORSE'S EARS CAN ROTATE 180°. EARS SHOW A CHANGE OF MOOD.

2. EARS PRICKED FORWARD SHOW ALL ATTENTION IS FOCUSED IN ONE DIRECTION.

3. A HAPPY FACE.

4. EARS PINNED BACK IS A THREAT: "GO AWAY OR I'LL BITE."

5. EARS FLICKING RAPIDLY BACK AND FORTH: "I'M NERVOUS AND READY TO RUN."

6. EARS SIDEWAYS: "I QUIT, OR I'M GOING TO ACT STUBBORN."

7. DROOPY EARS: "I'M TIRED, BORED OR IN PAIN."

NOSE AND LIPS

8. NOSTRILS WIDE OPEN: "I'M EXCITED" OR "I'VE BEEN RUNNING AND I NEED MORE AIR."

9. TIGHT LIPS: "I'M NERVOUS OR IN PAIN."

10. FLEHMEN FACE, CURLING UPPER LIP: SOMETHING SMELLS GOOD OR STRANGE.

MOUTH

11. TEETH CHAMPING—
    MOUTH OPENS AND
    TEETH CLACK TO-
    GETHER: FOALS USE
    THIS TO SAY, "DON'T
    HURT ME, I'M ONLY A
    BABY."

12. LOWER LIP HANGING:
    "I'M TIRED OR RE-
    LAXED."

13. TONGUE OUT OF
    MOUTH. WHEN RUN-
    NING, IT MEANS, "I'M
    EXHAUSTED." IF AT
    REST, THE HORSE IS RE-
    LAXED.

HEAD

14. TOSSING HEAD UP AND
    DOWN: FRUSTRATED
    OR ANNOYED AND SIG-
    NALING YOU TO GO
    AWAY.

15. TWISTING HEAD FROM
    SIDE TO SIDE: "LET'S
    PLAY" OR "I'M READY
    FOR BATTLE."

16. LOUD SNORT:
    "WHAT'S THAT?"

17. TWO HORSES MEETING
    NOSE TO NOSE:
    "HELLO, WHO ARE
    YOU?"

EYES

18. HORIZONTAL PUPIL FOR SEEING AROUND THEM.

19. WHITE OF EYE SHOWING: "I'M SCARED." IF AN APPALOOSA, THE WHITE AROUND THE PUPIL MAY BE A BREED CHARACTERISTIC.

20. EYE HALF-CLOSED: HORSE IS DROWSY, RELAXED OR ILL. CHECK OTHER SIGNS FOR GENERAL ATTITUDE.

LEGS

21. STAMPING WITH FRONT OR BACK LEG: IRRITATED AT A PERSON OR FLIES.

22. PAWING. "LET'S GO! I'M TIRED OF WAITING!"

23. RAISED FRONT LEG: "BE CAREFUL, I MIGHT STRIKE YOU."

24. RAISED BACK LEG: "WATCH OUT. I MAY KICK."

TAIL

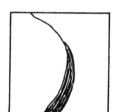

25. TAIL HIGH AND RAISED: "I'M HAPPY OR EXCITED."

26. TAIL LOW: "I'M TIRED, SCARED, ILL OR COLD."

27. SWISHING TAIL: "I'M NERVOUS OR UNHAPPY."

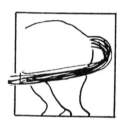

28. BIG SWISH: "LOOK OUT! I'M REALLY MAD."

BODY LANGUAGE

29. HORSE-TO-HORSE GROOMING: "LET'S BE FRIENDS."

30. BODY CHECK: LEAD HORSE CHARGES IN FRONT OF ONE LOWER IN THE PECKING ORDER.

31. SHOULDER PUSH: IF BODY CHECK DIDN'T WORK, LEAD HORSE PUSHES OTHER HORSE OUT OF THE WAY.

32. RUMP SWING: "I MAY KICK."

BLM Wild Horse and Burro Specialist John Winnepenninkx related, "The people who have real problems either give up too soon, lose interest in the horse, don't put the necessary time into it or else they didn't have the right facilities in the first place. It is more a dedication problem than a problem with the horses."

The director of the Eastern States Adopt-A-Horse office in Alexandria, Virginia, Curt Jones, said, "The ones I heard from that had troubles either rushed through or skipped the groundwork. But the public really likes the wild horses. They're smart and can be very good-looking. People are beginning to realize the potential and variety of uses for these horses."

These first days with your new horse are important in the bonding process, and in the gentling and training of your horse. The trust that you develop during this time will affect your entire relationship with your horse.

Some horses will accept human companionship in just a few hours, while others will take many weeks. Although we call these lessons Day One, they may occupy a single day or several weeks. Be patient. We have found that even with horses who require an exceptionally long period to bond, once it is accomplished, saddle or other training is easily done. These lessons are the foundation of your training program.

9.

THE FIRST TOUCH

One of the strongest instincts in a horse is the flight reflex. Frightened horses want to run. If they can't, they will bunch together, with heads and necks crisscrossed, touching and reassuring one another.

From birth, horses are taught to use touching to send messages and to use body contact to stimulate or comfort each other. If a foal is frightened, it runs to its mother. She will nuzzle it, saying in effect, "It's okay. I'm here. You're safe."

The captured wild horse in your corral is alone, maybe for the first time. His mother and other band members aren't there, and he no longer has a place in a pecking order. The horse is undoubtedly feeling very insecure.

Besides the loss of his companions and having someone to follow, all of the horse's daily routines are gone as well. He has only his emotions and instincts to depend on, instincts that say humans are very dangerous—stay as far away from them as possible.

Up to now, your calm actions have been building on a foundation of trust. You have been showing the horse that you are not going to attack or hurt it. Touching is the next bonding lesson in sending a message of safety and protection to your horse, rekindling his feelings of security.

Touch is essentially talking with your hands. Yet to apply your hands or any other part of your body to the horse, you obviously need to be near the horse.

TECHNIQUES FOR GETTING CLOSE

As discussed in chapter 8, getting close to a wild horse without panicking him is an exercise in advance, stop, and advance again or retreat, depending on the horse's reaction. As you move closer, you will be stepping into your horse's flight space, so approaching will take time.

By now your horse should be comfortable with you standing in the center of the corral. Stand quietly, talking to your horse until he is calmed down and settled. When the horse is looking at you,

CHINA LAKE BOOMER IS GIVING HIS FULL ATTENTION TO THE "WATCH ME" COMMAND. BARBARA LOWERS HER BODY TO PROJECT A LESS THREAT-ENING ATTITUDE.

repeat the command "Watch me." By this time the horse should be comfortable and responding to your vocal instructions and body language. When the horse is watching you in a relaxed manner, ears pointed toward you and eyes focused on you, advance by taking a step toward him, at a right angle to the middle of his body.

He may be frightened by this new action on your part, so stop and wait until he is relaxed and calm again. Keep up a steady stream of talk, soft and low, to reassure the horse. If the horse's attention starts to wander, vary your vocal sound, for example, with a low whistle. Remember not to use cues you may have used to make him go forward, such as the clucking sound. Repeat until you are close enough to extend your hand within a few inches of the horse's nose. Slowly extend your hand. Stop and let the horse accept this before advancing again. The horse may jump forward, so be sure to allow him an avenue of escape.

If at any point the horse panics and runs around the corral, go back to the center of the corral and start over. The point of this lesson is to convice the horse to come to you willingly, of its own choice.

A technique that animal communication specialist Penelope Smith uses with very frightened, panicky animals and young horses at shows is to point at something away from the animal, saying, "Look at that."

After the horse looks, she acknowledges by saying "Thank you" or "Good boy." Then she points to something else, repeating "Look at that." She repeats this five to ten times, until the horse is calmed down. She feels that this exercise helps focus the horse's attention on something outside himself and allows him to regain control of his emotions. You might try and see if this technique works on your horse. If you use this method, you will need to bring the horse's attention back to you before you continue the lesson. Also, make sure the horse does not confuse this action with your body signal to go forward. If the horse appears confused, pick another cue to break his concentration. The key is to redirect the horse's attention. Other methods—such as low whistling, changing your voice pattern, snapping your fingers, moving the horse forward—can be used to change the horse's focus from something that is frightening him back to you.

Starting again with the horse, you should be able to get close to him somewhat faster this time. It all depends on how frightened and threatened the horse is feeling by your being close.

ORPHAN FOALS AT THE LIFE EQUINE CENTER. FOLLOWING A LEADER IS A STRONG INSTINCT IN HORSES. (PHOTO BY BARBARA EUSTIS-CROSS)

This may take tremendous patience on your part, but that's what is necessary to gentle and educate a wild horse. Your time and patience will be rewarded down the road, when you have established a bond with your horse.

When this happens, the horse will look to you for leadership. Following a new leader, the horse will feel more secure.

Older wild horses (five years and up) that have been leaders of their own bands may resent having to step down from being boss. Techniques to use with dominant, aggressive horses will be presented later in this chapter.

EMOTIONS ARE IMPORTANT

If you are working with your horse and find yourself getting angry, impatient or tired, quit for a while. One minute of hasty anger can ruin hours or weeks of patient work. If you end the lesson with a pleasant feeling, the horse will look forward to your company and the next lesson.

Come back for your next lesson when you are in a more cheerful frame of mind. Your thoughts and inner emotions are every bit as important as what you are saying or doing with your voice and body. The horse will sense how you are feeling and react accordingly. If you are saying "Come here, sweetie pie, darling" but thinking "Get over here, you stupid blockhead," the horse won't be fooled. As you approach the horse, focus on some easy gentle thoughts or think about something funny.

Enjoy yourself. The horse will pick up on your emotion and want to enjoy itself, too. When you see someone laughing, you ask, "What's so funny?" because you want to laugh, too. We're all more receptive when we're in a good mood.

Horses definitely have a sense of humor. They like to play jokes on each other. If one horse has a broken halter, another will have fun tugging on the strap or leading the poor horse around with it. Some horses think ripping each other's blankets is great fun.

Horse handling doesn't have to be deadly serious, but you should stay alert to the horse's body language to see if his mood is changing. Watch the horse's reactions carefully. Learn to read your horse's signals like a road map that tells you what direction to go. You need to know a horse's red light from his yellow or green light. It's better to be near a horse when he's flashing a green light, rather than a red. If it is yellow, wait! Be cautious until the horse gives a clear indication of what he is feeling and willing to do.

Continue with your advance, stop, advance again or retreat, until you are close enough to touch the horse. This may come in a few hours or it could take several weeks, depending on the horse's personality and if he has been seriously frightened or injured during roundup or captivity.

Don't force the issue. Eventually it will happen, so don't make a big deal out of it. Be very casual, as if touching the horse would be nice for both of you but isn't that important. Remember, you want to keep the pressure off the horse. If the horse becomes too nervous or frightened, back off. Try again later, easing up to him little by little. If the horse is calm and curious, then keep going and make the connection—touch the horse.

No-nonsense horses may be more willing to let you get close if you are holding out a handful of hay. If that works with your horse,

THE FIRST TOUCH—EVENTUALLY IT WILL HAPPEN!

try withholding his morning hay ration a half hour before you go in, so the horse will be more eager to accept your close presence with the additional bonus of breakfast.

THE FIRST TOUCH

There are different schools of thought on what part of the horse to touch first. Some say touch the face first, others say start at the neck, shoulder or barrel. During an interview, Lyn Kamer said, "I started with the face, muzzle and forehead area. These are areas that are used to contact other members of the equine family."

Robin Rivello's first touch was on the nose, because every time she would approach her horse from the side, the horse would swing around to face her.

Some horse trainers contend that a horse's striking reflex, the instinct to attack with his front legs, may be set off by contact in the nose area. The authors have never seen this but warn that it never is a good idea to stand directly in front of a horse or in such a way that if he panics he will knock you off balance or down.

Many people have found that first touching the neck, withers, shoulder or barrel is most comfortable for the horse. The area on the neck just in front of the withers is a very sensitive area. You can often observe horses grooming each other there. This is the way a mare reassures her frightened foal. Moving your fingertips in a clockwise motion simulates equine body language; it says to the horse, "You are safe with me."

READ THE HORSES'S BODY LANGUAGE TO DETERMINE ON WHICH PART OF THE BODY IT WILL FIRST ACCEPT CONTACT.

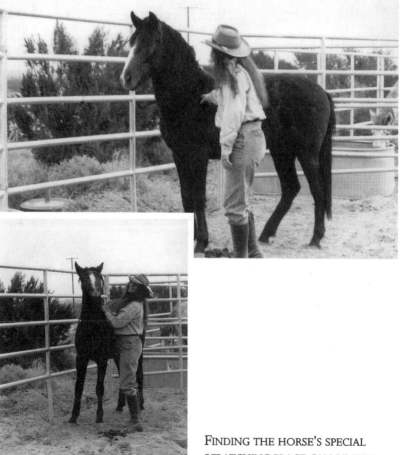

FINDING THE HORSE'S SPECIAL SCRATCHING PLACE CAN BE FUN.

Every horse has an especially sensitive area where he likes to be touched. Once your horse is used to you handling him, you will know when you have found your horse's "spot." His lips may start to quiver and extend out, his body may lean toward you, or he may simply display signs of relaxing.

The side of the horse is a natural neutral zone. Appear from the front and the horse will back up. Appear from the rear and the horse will go forward. But if you approach at the side of the horse, about two-thirds of the way up from the tail, the horse doesn't have an impulse to go forward or backward.

Experiment with each of the above, all the while reading your horse's signals to see what is working. Most likely the horse will move away or back up on your first try, but give him time to realize he is not going to be hurt, then calmly touch again. Spend time talking to the horse and reassuring him.

Too much too soon can overwhelm your horse and cause him to try to escape the physical and emotional pressure he is feeling.

Take your time, keeping in mind that this slow period will not last forever. These are the little blocks that, one at a time, will become the foundation of your entire relationship with your horse.

Don't expect your horse to learn everything overnight. Teach one thing at a time and give him a chance to understand.

CLOSER CONTACT

When the horse allows you to keep touching him without a fuss, bring your own body close and use both hands on his body, slowly and in a caressing way, in the direction the hair lies. Try moving your hands slowly up the horse's mane, speaking quietly.

The next step is to place your arm over the horse's back and put some gentle pressure on your arm. This simulates the comforting action of another horse, such as when frightened horses bunch together. The horse's back is a very vulnerable spot, where, in the horse's ancestral past, lions or other predators would attack and kill, leaping down from above. This lesson will give you a good indication if the horse accepts you as a natural part of his life, with a place in the pecking order, or if you are still an outsider.

THE NEXT STEP IS TO PLACE AN ARM OVER THE HORSE'S BACK AND PUT SOME GENTLE PRESSURE ON YOUR ARM.

BARBARA BLOCKS THE FORWARD MOVEMENT OF THIS COLT AS SHE WORKS WITH HIS HEAD, NECK AND EYES.

Another action horses use with each other during friendly grooming sessions is nibbling each other's manes. You can imitate this by using your thumb and fingers as a horse would use his teeth. Use your fingers to gently "nibble" the horse's mane up and down the crest of the neck.

When the horse accepts this contact, continue to run your hands over other parts of the body. Work from head to tail, praising the horse as you work. Sometimes a horse will accept a light brushing with a soft brush more readily than the feel of hands.

Be aware of the horse's body signals. If the horse moves away, let him go. You want the horse to *voluntarily* allow you to come close without forcing him. The horse needs the psychological freedom to be able to move away if he wants to.

A horse generally feels more comfortable being touched on one side or the other of his body. While one horse may tolerate you touching his right shoulder from the beginning, he may constantly move away as you reach that same area on the left side. Like people, horses are right- or left-sided. If a horse is decidedly uneasy with you working on one side, then work on the other. Later, as the horse has more trust in you, come back and work with the more difficult side, where you may have to go slower, as the horse needs time to build confidence in you being there. In later training, work both sides of the horse, spending more time on the horse's less favorite side.

It will help if you introduce the command "Stand" during this lesson. Each time you approach the horse to touch him, repeat the command, then reward the horse with a favorite scratch. If the horse begins to move away, repeat the command. Usually your voice will bring the horse's attention back to you and he will stop moving.

TOUCHING THE HEAD

As the horse becomes comfortable with you touching him, you will want to spend extra time on his head area. Practice gentle movements and strokes on the head, including around and on the ears. Horses are very sensitive about their ears. Head shyness or not wanting their head and/or ears touched, is a common problem with horses that have not been handled properly in the beginning, and it can turn into a life-long problem. One reason is that the horse's primary danger detectors—the eyes, ears and nose—are in this area.

If the horse becomes tense when you're touching his head, you may want to start scratching or rubbing the neck right before the withers and gradually move your way up the mane. As the horse accepts this, slowly move your hands to the ears. If the horse resists, throwing up his head or pinning his ears, he is trying to say, "Stop, you are going too fast." Move your hands to another area where he does enjoy contact, and gradually work your way back to the ears.

You may want to investigate the TT.E.A.M. methods of touching taught by Linda Tellington-Jones, which can be very helpful in establishing good communication with your horse. (TT.E.A.M. can be reached at P.O. Box 3793, Sante Fe, New Mexico 87501-03793.)

Next, begin touching the halter, by sliding your fingers around and under the strap areas. Be sure you do not put your fingers so far into the straps that an unexpected movement from the horse would allow your fingers to be caught in the halter.

Next, try moving the horse's head from side to side with your hand on his cheek. If the horse resists, do not force the lesson. Little pressures may be more effective than a long, drawn-out push. Continue these lessons until the horse is reconciled about you touching all parts of his head and ears and will allow you to move the head from side to side. When this is accomplished, handle the halter area below the jaw where you attach the dragline. You want the horse to get used to your handling this area and touching the dragline.

THE DIFFICULT HORSE

A small percentage of horses will not come along as smoothly as this despite your best intentions and efforts. More aggressive, dominant horses may be threatened by your coming close. These horses need to be dealt with in a different manner, firmly but not cruelly. Cruelty, force and physical blows will only push them to become mean. Mistreated horses may eventually submit but will never willingly give themselves.

If you find yourself with a horse that consistently turns his rear end to you, it is a simple matter to make him uncomfortable without being violent. Remove the rounded corners from the corral so you again have four square corners. You will need a longe or buggy whip at least 65 inches long and a small plastic bag or a long stiff rope such as a lariat. Tie the plastic bag onto the whip. Enter the corral in a confident manner. The horse will probably run to the farthest point possible from you and end up with his head pointed into a corner.

Give the horse a moment to calm down. Do not stand directly behind the horse, and make sure you are not within striking distance. Point the whip end or toss the lariat at the horse's rear end, on the side opposite the direction you want the horse to travel. The horse will most likely kick at the offending object and bolt to the next corner. Repeat until the horse finally stops kicking and bolting.

Soon the horse will turn around and look at you with an expression of "What do you want?" Or he may just stop moving and show you an attitude of "Now what?" The horse is now communicating with you, is now "willingly giving" to you on his own. Use this time to talk to the horse, to blow at it, and, if he will allow, to approach slowly. As soon as the horse starts to look at you, use the command "Watch me." If the horse bolts again, allow him to settle and repeat the command.

Repeat the lesson until the horse responds to the command. The whole process should take less than sixty minutes, and in most cases the horse will not turn his rear end to you again. The next day, walk into the corral, let the horse settle and give the command. With luck, your horse will turn to look at you. If not, repeat the lesson.

A horse that rears and strikes at you (like a boxer throwing a punch) or strikes from the ground is an aggressive animal and should be handled only by a professional or experienced handler. This is a rare occurrence, but it is mentioned to let you know that some horses, usually ones mishandled by people, have acted this way.

EMERGENCY METHODS

When you must touch the horse right away for medical or other reasons, here is a method to try if the horse still has the dragline on. You will need two people, one on the outside of the corral and one on the inside. Both people should be wearing gloves to protect their hands. Have a longe or buggy whip ready to use. First move the horse forward around the corral. Continue until the horse becomes tired, to the point of wanting to stop.

The outside person should be standing next to the post which is placed on the inside of the corral, midway along one of the corral panels (a panel of ¾-inch plywood, at least 4 feet high and 8 feet wide, should be attached to the corral on either side of the pole). The inside person will need to enter the corral and allow the horse to settle down. Move the horse forward until the end of the dragline is close to the post. Quietly pick up the end of the dragline and hand it to the outside person. The inside person should then move toward the front of the horse, so he won't bolt forward.

Allow plenty of room between you and the horse, or the horse will turn and run the other way. You are simply discouraging the horse from moving away from the post. The outside person will wrap the dragline *several* times around the post. The rope must be tied so it is higher than the horse's withers. *WARNING: Do not allow your fingers or hand to get between the rope and the post!* The horse will probably be fighting the rope now. The inside person should back off until the horse has calmed down.

When the horse is calm, the inside person can move forward, still far enough away from the horse to avoid the rear feet, but moving the horse toward the post. The inside person will be pulling the rope tighter until the horse's head is no more than 2 feet away from the post. The outside person should tie off the rope with a quick-release knot. The inside person should come out of the corral, and the outside person should back off away from the horse. Allow the horse time to fight the rope.

Wild animals do not want to waste energy by fighting when they realize they aren't going to get away. When the horse has calmed down, slowly approach him, talking calmly. When the horse has accepted you at this closer distance, slip the whip through the corral and touch him on the neck. This will probably cause a whole new outbreak of jumping, snorting and attempting to get away. Allow the horse to settle down and try again. Keep repeating until you can touch most parts of the body with the whip. Remember, you are using the whip as an extension of your hand—to gently touch the horse, not as a punishment. When the horse is comfortable with the whip touching him, start working on his face with your hands. Make sure your hands and arms are extended over the top of the plywood, so that if the horse moves you can move your hands freely and quickly.

This process may take several hours. Be patient and alternate people to give yourself a rest. Once the horse stays calm when you touch his face, untie it and begin immediately training as described earlier with the less aggressive horse. The horse will be very tired by now, and more anxious to just stand and allow you to approach him.

REWARDS

Some people like to introduce grain at this point, as an incentive for the horse to come close. Rewards for being cooperative help the horse to know he is doing what you want; they give the horse a happy experience. Practical horses enjoy a food reward, a handful of hay or grain. Wild horses may not know what grain is, and

ONE DAY YOUR HORSE MAY RE-GARD YOU AS ONE OF THE FAMILY!

many don't want to try it at first. You can sprinkle it on their hay to get them used to it. Go easy, though, no more than a pound a day to begin with, because the horse's system isn't used to it. Also the energy-producing effects of the grain could make your horse more frisky and harder to handle. After they sample it a few times, most horses love grain.

Rewarding a horse or convincing him to do what you want by offering him rewards gets fast results and certainly works. But it's also important to teach the horse to respond to your cues, commands and body language without the reward. It is important that your horse responds to you willingly and that it is comfortable with you and the lessons, rather than just accepting what you are asking him to do. There is a world of difference between the two.

Make it a point to touch your horse every time you bring his hay and water, for even a short ten minutes or so. By visiting the horse often, feeding and gentling him, the day will soon come when the horse regards you as a member of his family. One morning the horse will walk over to greet you or whinny hello, and you can feel justifiably proud of a job well done. You have become the friend of a wild horse.

10.

HALTER AND LEAD ROPE TRAINING

In the early weeks, keep in mind that you're still a stranger to your horse and that he will continue to be cautious of your actions.

When you're introducing a new lesson and the horse is afraid, he may resist to protect himself or because he's not sure what you are asking him to do. Resistance, repeated a few times in a row, can become a bad habit that is tough to overcome.

Set up your lessons so it is easier for the horse to do the right thing and uncomfortable or harder for him to do the wrong thing. You have already done this in previous lessons. Running away from you in the corral became tiring for the horse, but standing and allowing you to talk to him or touch him was a pleasant experience.

A horse handled properly will work with people willingly, because he has learned to have confidence. However, a horse that is overpowered and forced to submit becomes a mindless, unhappy slave. Your main goal should be to reduce the horse's fears by being patient and to give the horse time to understand each new thing before starting a new lesson.

The horse cannot be expected to completely understand human beings in a few weeks. Most of us have been human for quite some time now and still can't understand half the things our families do or say! Keep this in mind when you're teaching your human ways, signals and language to a completely different type of being.

You can ease the horse into learning by giving him good experiences when you are with him by providing food, water, and companionship (a horse alone is a lonely horse).

Since you have brought your horse home he has learned:

• To accept someone entering the corral to bring food and water and to clean up.
• Not to run away when you approach.
• To turn and face you on the command "Watch me."
• To stand still and allow you to touch his face, neck, shoulders, ears and the halter and dragline.
• The voice command "Stand."

The next step will be halter and lead training, which is teaching your horse to:

• Lead, or walk beside you on a rope.
• Understand the commands "Walk," "Whoa" and "Back."
• Stand tied without a fuss.
• Allow the halter to be taken off and put on again.

LEADING

When you begin to teach the horse to lead, you are simply transferring to you his natural instinct to follow another horse. Before you start, check the dragline to make sure it's not frayed or weak in any place. Pay special attention to the areas where the horse has been stepping on the rope.

If the rope isn't in good shape, replace it with a new one. Your horse is relaxed when you work around his head now, so this should not be difficult. Recheck your corral, too, for weak or loose boards, and nails or sharp edges that could hurt you or the horse.

If your horse is not familiar with another person in or around the corral, now is a good time to introduce someone besides you. You will need an assistant sooner or later, and it's best to bring someone in when all he or she will be doing is standing around.

In the beginning, the assistant should stand on the same side of the horse as you are, so that the horse will not become nervous as he attempts to keep an eye on both of you.

Here are several things to remember as you teach your horse to lead:

- Never wrap the rope, or lead, around your hand. Always gather the rope so it lies inside your palm, with your fingers on the outside.
- Avoid standing directly in front of the horse; otherwise you may get trampled if the horse panics and jumps forward.
- Do not allow the rope to drag around your legs, where you could become caught in it.
- Always allow the untrained horse an avenue of escape.
- Walk your horse on the left side, but sometimes practice leading on the right.
- Hold the rope in the left hand, with your right hand free.
- Use your right hand for firmer control, by holding the rope below where it attaches to the halter.
- You may also use your right hand on the neck or shoulder, to maintain the distance between you and the horse if he crowds or jumps toward you.
- Wear gloves!

Standing on the left side of the horse, pick up the dragline with your left hand. Step back, guiding the horse's head in your direction. This will be a review of earlier lessons. When the horse responds, start walking in a large circle, turning toward the horse's hindquarters.

Your pressure on the dragline, and your body language, should direct the horse to follow as you make a bigger circle. As the circle widens, go in a straight path for a short way. If the horse hesitates or refuses to go forward, use your hand on the dragline to guide his head, turning it to the right while using your body to guide his body into the turn.

If the horse still hesitates, continue to go in a circle. A horse will follow his head, so if you have control of the head, the horse's body must follow. When the horse becomes bored with going in a circle, he will appreciate going forward again.

"WHOA," "WALK" AND "BACK"

Practice turning left and right and walking in figure eights.

An assistant walking behind the horse, far out of kicking range, will also encourage the horse to go forward, if he's having trouble understanding what you want.

If you don't have an assistant, it may help to use a long stiff whip about 4 feet long, such as a dressage whip. First get the horse used to the whip, by letting him see and smell it; then stroke his body all over with it.

Hold the whip in your left hand, with a little extra slack in the dragline, and give the command "Walk." At the same time, bring the whip behind you and tap LIGHTLY on the horse's croup. Although awkward at first, by giving the "Walk" command and facing forward, your body language is telling the horse to move, while the tap also encourages him.

Another way some trainers teach their horses to go forward is by putting a longe line or a long rope around the horse's rump and then back to the trainer's hand. The idea is that the pressure from behind will cause the horse to move ahead.

Be careful not to pull the horse forward. Just give the "Walk" command, and let the rope do the work. It should only take a few times for the horse to realize what to do.

Yet, if the horse is still skittish about being touched, this method wouldn't be a good idea. The horse could rocket forward, knocking you down in the process.

Other horses may refuse to go forward and may back up instead. If the horse does this, turn to face the horse (remember to stand slightly to the side, away from the horse's body) while holding the rope directly under the halter.

Give the rope a pull downward and back toward the horse while saying the command "Back." This will startle the horse, and his natural reaction will be to move away from you. Continue to say "Back," giving a tug on the halter if necessary. When the horse hesitates, stop, turn and give the command "Walk" while turning the horse to the right. Your horse should appreciate going forward now.

ANOTHER WAY TO TEACH YOUR HORSE TO GO FORWARD IS TO PUT A LONG
LINE AROUND ITS BODY.

As you're leading your horse, teach him to stop or halt by saying
a quiet, drawn-out "Whoa" (pronounced HO) and stopping your
own motion. At the same time, give a short pull-and-release signal
on the halter. Praise the horse when he stops, then repeat the
lesson.

Begin again with the "Walk" command. Practice the transition
from walk to halt a few times until the horse gets a firm idea of
what you're asking.

If at some point the horse refuses to move, don't try to pull him
foward. It's impossible for a human to win a tug-of-war with a
horse! Instead, turn the horse in a circle until he is moving freely.

On the other hand, if the horse ever tries to bolt away from you,
turn his head toward you while moving away from the horse's
body. Short give-and-take pulls on the rope work better to slow
the horse down than a long, continuous pull. The horse will always
be stronger and will win the pulling contest. Try to be flexible
enough that you can handle your horse even when he's not being
cooperative.

During lessons, be aware of the horse's attention span. Young horses are like children: when they get bored, learning sags. Short lessons are best. If you stop on a good note, your horse may even look forward to the next time you will work together.

Practice these two leading lessons during the next few days, until you have smooth transitions from walking to stop and back again. You can start this next lesson when the horse is comfortable with you handling the dragline.

Give the command "Stand," then, while facing the horse, step back a few paces. Move and swing the dragline back and forth, as if you were playing an easy game of jump rope.

The horse may try to come toward you or go backward. If so, return the horse to his original position and repeat the command until the horse accepts the movement of the rope without moving.

Then you can take the end of the rope and toss it gently on the horse's chest, sides, back and neck. This exercise is similar to sacking out, the method some trainers use prior to saddle training. A soft burlap sack or a saddle blanket is gently slapped all over the

THE DRAGLINE IS BEING GENTLY SWUNG LIKE A JUMP ROPE, TO GET THE HORSE MOVING ON A LEAD.

horse's body. This is done to get him used to being touched in different areas and also to accept movement around his body.

Another good lesson is teaching the horse to walk with a rope around his neck. This is rather simple once your horse is willingly walking beside you. Start by draping a light rope over the horse's neck. As you walk forward, keep directing the horse with the dragline in your left hand. With your right hand, guide the horse with the neck rope.

Then try guiding the horse only with the neck rope. This lesson will come in handy if your horse ever has a broken halter or bridle and you need to walk him home.

When this is old hat, bring in a regular 10-foot lead rope. Let the horse see the new rope and touch and sniff it. Quietly stroke the horse's body with the rope, to show that it's harmless and to put the horse's scent on it. As the horse accepts this, click the snap a few times, until the horse is not nervous with the sound. Place the dragline over the horse's neck, holding it in your left hand to control the horse, while putting on the new lead line with the right hand. When the lead line is secure, remove the dragline.

Take a few steps, then give the command "Whoa" and the stop cue of a short, firm pull on the lead line. Walk around the corral, practicing stopping and starting as you did before.

LETTING THE HORSE GET ACCUS-TOMED TO MOVEMENT AROUND THE BODY IS IMPORTANT FOR LATER TRAINING.

Learning any new skill or exercise is awkward in the beginning, so remember to give your equine student plenty of praise when it does what you ask.

STANDING TIED

After you have accomplished the above lessons, it's time to teach the horse to stand tied. This is where your sturdy pole will be used. For these first lessons, never tie the horse to a board in a fence. A hysterical horse galloping around attached to a flapping board is not a pretty sight! At this time, it's also important to check your halter for any weak spots. Make sure you don't use a break-away halter for this lesson.

Tie a lead rope to the post, using a quick-release hitch knot, at a height slightly above the horse's withers. The lead rope needs to be tied to provide a space of about 24 inches from the pole to where the horse's head will be tied.

If the lead rope is too long, the horse could get a leg over it; if it's too short, the horse may feel trapped and panic. Don't let the end of the lead rope lie all over the ground.

An important warning: never use a stud chain or a lead with a chain end for this lesson, because it doesn't have the strength to securely hold your horse if he acts up. Also, never place this type of lead over any horse's nose when he is tied up. The pressure that is exerted when the horse is pulling back could break the delicate nose bones.

For these tie lessons, some trainers recommend tying the horse to an inner tube that is attached to the pole. The rubber will stretch, lessening the strain on the horse's neck when he pulls back.

To start, lead your horse over to the pole, and spend a few minutes brushing the horse and talking. Casually clip on the rope attached to the post. Remove the lead line. As the horse stands quietly, say "Stand" and praise the horse.

Walk away calmly. When the horse tries to follow or realizes he can't leave, he will probably struggle with the rope. The response can range from a few head tosses to an all-out war!

1. MAKE A WRAP OF THE FREE END OF YOUR ROPE AROUND A SECURE POST, OR TREE OR WHATEVER.

2. PASS THE FREE END OF THE ROPE OVER THE EXTENDED END, MAKE A LOOP AND PASS THE FREE END BACK UNDER THE EXTENDED ROPE.

3. REACH THROUGH THE LOOP AND DRAW A SMALL LOOP OF THE FREE END OF THE ROPE THROUGH IT.

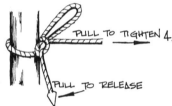

4. HOLD THE SECOND LOOP AND DRAW THE KNOT TIGHT WITH THE EXTENDED END OF THE ROPE.

5. THE KNOT IS RELEASED BY PULLING THE FREE END OF THE ROPE. TO PREVENT THE HORSE FROM RELEASING HIMSELF, PASS THE FREE END OF THE ROPE THROUGH THE REMAINING LOOP.

THE QUICK-RELEASE KNOT.

Let the horse test the rope and don't intervene. The horse will soon understand that this is a losing battle and stop fighting. If a problem develops and the horse throws himself down, attempt to get the horse up without untying the rope. If you must untie the rope, simply pull the end of the quick-release hitch knot.

While the horse is tied for the first time, putter around the corral, cleaning up, filling buckets, reading a book or whatever. The point is to remain unruffled. Don't feel sorry for the horse. This is a lesson that he must learn.

After the horse has accepted being tied and is standing calmly, leave him alone for a few minutes. Later, go back and praise and reward your horse, showing him how happy you are with him.

Now put your lead line back on, remove the pole rope, and walk the horse away from the area before releasing him. Never let the horse go directly from the pole. That would teach him that he can immediately escape, and some day you may find yourself on the ground wondering what happened.

If the horse has gotten loose because of a broken halter or lead pole, or if you have had to untie him for any reason, it's important to tie the horse again after he has settled down. You will probably have to go slower, perhaps standing by the pole with the horse untied for a while, munching on hay, before retying and starting over.

In the next few weeks, practice tying the horse for different periods of time, to get him used to standing patiently. Leave the horse alone where he cannot see or hear you, so he will become accustomed to being on good behavior even if you are not around.

TAKING THE HALTER ON AND OFF

By now, your horse should have confidence in you and be less likely to bolt or run off the minute the halter is removed.

To begin, move your hands all around the horse's head and ears, under his chin, and in the space around the head. Handle the different parts of the halter, too. Slide your hand under the crown piece, the top strap of the halter behind the ears. Move the crown piece up and down, as if you were going to remove the halter, but don't do it just yet.

"Nibble" with your fingers up the horse's mane, and gradually touch gently around the ears. Next, take an old halter and let the horse examine it, a look-see and a sniff, then rub the halter on the body. Lift it up by the sides of the horse's head, in the same action you use when sliding the halter over the nose to put it on.

The horse has good side vision, so go slow, because sudden movements might startle him. Hold the halter over one side of the neck and jiggle it around. Praise the horse whenever he is standing quietly. If he objects to anything, wait. Go back to working on something the horse has accepted.

Without actually buckling the halter, keep putting the old halter over the one still on the horse until the horse is comfortable with the action.

Then place the lead line over the horse's neck, leading him or her around for a few minutes, so the horse's attention is transferred from the halter to the neck area.

PRACTICE MOVING YOUR HANDS AROUND THE HORSE'S HEAD AND GET IT USED TO GENTLE STROKING AROUND THE EARS.

IT'S A GOOD IDEA TO PRACTICE SLIP-PING THE HALTER ON AND OFF.

While still holding the lead line with your left hand, remove the halter. Say "Stand" and repeat the halter lesson, until the horse accepts the halter being put on and off without objection.

Give the horse a gentle scratch in the areas where the halter lays on the face. The horse will probably appreciate it, because of the pressure from the halter being there. You know how good it feels to rub your nose after you take glasses off!

If the horse gets the notion to pull away, you will still have control with the neck rope. You don't want the horse to feel he can escape from you. Once the horse is standing quietly, give the command "Stand" and start the lesson over.

When the horse is agreeable about you taking the halter on and off, practice in different areas of the corral. It is important for the horse to stand after the halter has been taken off. By doing that, the horse avoids getting into the nasty habit of dashing away the second the halter is unbuckled.

If the horse does run off, repeat the first lessons of moving the horse around the corral. Stand in the center and give the command "Watch me." When you have the horse's attention, tell him to "Stand."

Now approach the horse, halter in hand. Don't get into the game of hiding the halter. Slip the lead rope over the neck and put the halter on.

If the horse continues to be disagreeable, move him around the corral in a brisk manner, until it is more pleasant to stand with you and have the halter put on than to keep going around and around like a carousel horse.

As the horse learns this lesson, you may want to practice teaching him to follow you without a lead, using the horse's natural impulse to follow a leader.

For your horse's future life outside the corral, it's a good idea to teach him to come when you call. Start teaching the horse to respond to his name from the beginning.

Every time you walk out to the corral greet your horse by name and use his name as often as possible during training. Practice calling the horse to you when you first walk into the corral.

You may need to give the command "Watch me" first, and then offer a handful of grain or hay as you call the horse. Replace the food with a physical reward like a scratch or a rub as soon as possible.

If at some point you are having problems with your horse misunderstanding what you want, use your overloaded brain and try to figure out what may be going wrong.

- Are you introducing too much at once?
- Are you using sudden or fast movements?
- Keep an eye on the horse's signals—ears, nose and legs—to try to learn what emotion the horse is feeling: fear, anger or confusion.
- Remember to work on both sides of the horse. Be aware that one side may be slower than the other.
- Some horses take longer to accept new things.

11

THE MIGHTY HOOF

In the wild, the horse's primary defense against predators is his feet, for both running away and attacking. Thus horses are understandably nervous about anyone touching or handling their legs and feet.

When teaching your horse to give you his feet, it helps to remember three R's: relax, reassure and repeat. That is, to be relaxed but aware when working around the legs and feet, to reassure your horse when he's frightened, and, if the horse becomes tense, to repeat the first two!

ADVANCE AND RETREAT

Preparing to handle the feet can begin as you are educating the horse to accept your hands on his body. Stand next to the horse, facing the tail, and touch the shoulder area. Let your hand move down toward the front or side of the leg.

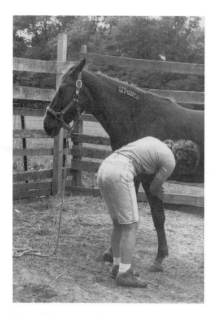

To lift the hoof, run your hand down the leg.

For the first time, bringing the leg forward is more acceptable to some horses.

If the horse starts to tense up or move away from you, bring your hand back up to the shoulder and resume rubbing or scratching there. Continue this "advance and retreat" until your horse is comfortable with you touching his front leg down to the knee.

When your horse is not actively resisting your touch, move your hand toward the back of the leg. Most horses will now step forward and/or lift the leg.

Gently take hold of the leg. Give the command "Foot" or "Hoof, please." Let the leg go when the horse starts to resist. Eventually when you give the command, the horse will offer you his leg by picking it up himself.

With this method, the horse's leg is brought forward instead of backward toward the knee in the usual way. Horses seem to offer less resistance to the forward movement, perhaps because it is a more natural action.

You will notice in the photograph that the mare is allowing the owner to bring her leg forward. Although the mare is concerned, note the alert expression on her face. She is letting the leg be lifted and not trying to move away. When this photograph was taken, the mare had about three hours of training since her capture.

With time and patience, the horse will let you move the front leg forward and backward. When the horse stays calm as you're holding the leg, try extending it forward.

It's better not to kneel by the horse's hooves in the beginning. If the horse becomes excited for any reason, you will have to move quickly. The safest place for you to stand is as close to the horse's body as he will allow. The farther away you stand, the better target you make for flying hooves.

When you feel the horse is ready to learn about his back legs, it's helpful to have an assistant holding the horse's head. The assistant can distract the horse at the front end while you're working at the back end.

Read your horse's body language to make sure you're not rushing him. While with a domestic horse the assistant usually stands on the opposite side of the trainer, with the untrained wild horse you should both work on the same side. This allows the horse an avenue of escape if he panics. Make sure the horse is used to having two people working around him. Remember, if one person is threatening to a wild horse, two are even more so.

If your horse is comfortable with you handling his head, here is a simple trick that seems to work with most horses. If you notice that the horse is becoming tense or is showing the white part of his eyes, make a loose fist and gently knock on the flat area between the eyes. DO NOT do this rapidly or in a violent manner, but rather as though you were knocking on the door of a sleeping friend. If you do it correctly, the horse will blink and refocus, trying to figure out what you're doing and forgetting his fear.

As you're working around the legs, let the horse get used to feeling your hands on his hindquarters, then start moving down to the thigh. Most horses will move ahead if you touch the back part of the thigh and go backward if you touch the front of the thigh.

At first, keep your other hand on the horse's hindquarters to detect any tensing of the muscles there. If you feel tension, the horse is starting to feel threatened, so stop and reassure him.

As the horse remains unruffled with you touching the hindquarters and thighs, move further down to the gaskin and hock

TAPPING THE HEAD LIGHTLY MAY GIVE YOU THE HORSE'S ATTENTION.

area. When the horse will stand quietly as you touch above the hock area, give the "Foot" command and gently hold the back leg forward for a few seconds.

Relax, reassure and repeat. This time extend your hand farther down the leg until you are past the hock, but not to the hooves yet. Any time the horse gets nervous, soothe him by scratching his favorite spots and talking in a low, comforting voice.

HANDLING THE HOOVES

Work every day on both sides of the horse, until you can handle all legs easily. When your horse is responding to the command "Foot" and is relaxed with two people around, it's time to begin picking up the legs and handling the hooves.

Standing close to the horse, facing the rear, run your left hand down the left front leg. Lean slightly into the horse's shoulder, asking him to shift his weight to the other side. Say "Foot," then with the left hand squeeze the fetlock.

As the horse begins to lift his foot, take hold of the hoof with the right hand. Hold the hoof for a few seconds, then carefully let the foot down. If you drop the foot suddenly, it will startle the horse. Praise the horse like Happy New Year if he's been cooperating.

If the horse tries to pull the hoof away, keep a light hold on the hoof until the horse stops trying. Once he stops, gently put the foot down. However, if the hoof slips out of your hand or the horse gets it away, just calmly ask for the hoof again. Don't fight over the hoof, but being persistant will help the horse realize that you're going to hold it no matter what.

If the horse doesn't respond right away to your commands and signals, don't assume he's being stubborn. The horse may not yet understand what you want him to do.

Another method to give the horse incentive to pick up his hoof is tickling the horse's heel just under the fetlock. This is a tender spot, and most horses will lift their hoof when touched there.

Still no luck? Try placing your arm parallel to the horse's leg, with your elbow inside the horse's front knee. Lean into the horse's shoulder. While giving the magic word "Foot," take hold of the

WITH THE LEFT HAND, SQUEEZE THE FETLOCK.

TICKLING THE HEEL.

fetlock hairs with an upward movement, while bending your elbow into the back of the horse's knee. Repeat until the horse understands and is readily giving you his foot on command.

Now work with the other side, keeping in mind that horses are more resistant on one side than the other. You may have to spend twice as long on the off side. Go slow, being casual about the whole thing.

When the horse is giving both front feet willingly, take a break. If the lesson has been a short one and the horse isn't stressed, you can go onto the back feet. If it's been a long lesson, leave the back feet until tomorrow.

If you are continuing the next day, review yesterday's leg handling. Each time use your voice command and hold the hoof a little longer. Don't forget to praise the horse.

Your horse should be comfortable by now with you touching his hindquarters, so picking up the back feet is simply the next step. With a horse that is nervous when you are back there—that kicks at you, pins his ears flat back (not just pointed back as when he's listening to you) or swishes his tail in an impatient manner—is not ready yet to have you handle his back feet.

Continue instead with relaxation and touching exercises until the horse allows you to run your hands on his hindquarters, gaskin and hock areas.

A MORE AGGRESSIVE PLAN

If after several days your horse refuses to relax and continues to kick, use a more aggressive plan. Tie the horse to the stout pole in your corral. Tie the horse's head 12 to 18 inches from the post. When the horse has accepted being tied up and is not struggling, it's time to begin.

You need a rope or lariat for this lesson. If you have some skill with a lariat, lightly throw a large loop over the horse's hindquarters, but do not pull the loop or tighten it. Allow it to simply lie on the horse's rump. Or you may use a long rope piece, ½ to 1 inch in diameter, tossing the rope over the horse's hindquarters.

PRIOR TO LIFTING THE BACK LEG, RUN YOUR HAND DOWN TO THE GASKIN AND HOCK AREA.

LIGHTLY THROW A LARGE LOOP OVER THE HORSE'S HINDQUARTERS.

Most likely the horse will kick at the rope or lariat. Ignore these actions. If you remain calm, the horse will eventually calm down as well.

Keep doing this until the horse does not object to the rope lying on his rump, back, sides or the back of his legs. If you are using a lariat, you may want to use the unlooped portion or loose end of the rope for the legs and sides.

When the horse is comfortable with the rope touching the rest of his body, lay a large, open circle on the ground next to the horse. Both ends must be open, so there is no chance of the loop tightening around the horse's foot.

Now encourage the horse to step sideways, until he places one foot in the loop. This may take several tries. When the horse is calmly standing in the loop, give the command "Foot" and pull the loop toward you. Expect a strong jerk, as the horse fights and kicks at the rope.

Again, stay calm. Let the foot down. Talk to the horse to reassure him.

Repeat the lesson until the horse will pick up his foot on command, with little prompting from the rope. Try working the leg with the rope—forward, backward and to the side. When the horse is willingly giving you his feet in all directions, you may again try handling the hindquarters, legs and feet as described above.

As with the front feet, it is often easier if the hind foot is brought forward during the first few times. If ever the horse moves suddenly, straighten the arm that you have placed on the horse's hindquarters. This will push you away from the horse and help you maintain your balance.

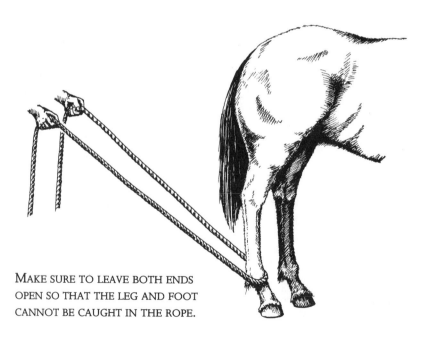

MAKE SURE TO LEAVE BOTH ENDS
OPEN SO THAT THE LEG AND FOOT
CANNOT BE CAUGHT IN THE ROPE.

THE FIRST TIME THIS MARE FELT THE ROPE ON HER FOOT, SHE KICKED VIO-
LENTLY AT THE ROPE.

BY THE THIRD ATTEMPT, THE MARE ACCEPTED THE ROPE ON HER FOOT.

AS YOU REACH THE CANNON BONE,
GENTLY PULL THE LEG FORWARD.
HOLD THE LEG UP A LITTLE LONGER
EACH TIME.

After you spend some time scratching and rubbing the hind-quarters area until the horse has relaxed, gradually move your hand farther down the leg again. As you reach the cannon bone, give the "Foot" command while gently pulling the leg forward.

If the horse gives to you by lifting or moving his leg, praise him and put the leg down. Repeat the lesson a few times, until the horse will let you bring the whole leg forward and also handle the hoof. Next, work with the leg and hoof being brought backward and sideways.

Lifting the feet will be part of your daily routine. Make it easier on everyone who will take care of your horse by teaching him with patience and good humor.

As you begin handling the feet for longer periods, you can introduce the hoof pick. Use the hoof pick, starting from the heel to the toe, scraping out any debris packed into the hoof on either side of the frog.

THE FARRIER

It will take the horse a while to learn to shift his weight and stand on three legs, so be patient. Once the horse is being a lady or gentleman about having his feet cleaned, then you can begin practicing for the farrier.

It is your responsibility to teach the horse to be well-mannered about his feet. Most farriers will not come out twice for an ill-tempered horse that puts them in danger of injury.

Work with your horse to accustom it to the actions used by the farrier when trimming or shoeing, such as:

- Stretching the front and hind legs forward.
- Placing the hoof between the knees.
- Tapping the hoof with a hoof pick to simulate the tapping in of nails.
- Holding the horse's tail to the side. If a horse flicks his tail across the face of the farrier, the razor-thin hairs can slice the eye, causing permanent damage.
- Practice having the horse balance on three legs for a long period of time.

All horses need their hooves trimmed at least every six to eight weeks. The time span depends on the ground your horse lives and works on, and how fast his hooves grow. Whether or not your horse needs horseshoes may be determined by several factors:

- Where will the horse be worked? Hard roads, rocky ground and heavy gravel areas call for shoes.
- If the horse is ridden lightly on soft ground or sandy areas, he may be better off barefoot.
- A horse that is turned out at pasture and not worked doesn't need shoes, unless he requires corrective shoeing. For safety reasons, it's better to leave shoes off young horses in group situations; during play, an iron horseshoe hurts more than a bare hoof. A kick from a shoed horse can cause serious damage.

. . .

LEARNING TO BALANCE ON THREE LEGS.

CALLIE THORNBURGH, CO-OWNER OF HIGH SIERRA TRAINING, HELPS PROTECT DAN BROWN'S FACE AND EYES BY HOLDING CINNAMON'S TAIL IN CASE SHE GETS IMPATIENT AND FLICKS IT.

Dan Brown, co-owner of High Sierra Training in Inyokern, California, is a professional trainer and farrier who handles the feet of performance and show horses, and also many former wild horses. The first time a farrier comes to do your horse, Brown suggests. "Give the horse a moderate workout in a round pen or working arena about an hour before the farrier arrives. This will settle the horse and get the nervous energy off. Let it rest a while, then work it a little more, until the horse is tired but not stressed. This will help make working on the horse easier."

This approach is a good example of making the right thing easy and the wrong thing uncomfortable. If your horse is tired, he will want to stand quietly and rest. Many of the little things that might have made the horse nervous before just won't be as important to a tired horse.

Each horse has hooves of unique shape and size. In some horses, not all the feet are the same shape or size. Some of the factors the farrier will consider before working on your horse are:

. . .

- How is your horse built? How much does he weigh?
- How will you be using this horse?
- What type of ground will he live and work on?
- What condition are the hooves in? Do they need corrective measures?

Every part of the horse's hoof is important and will affect how the horse moves and even his general condition and health. The wall of the hoof helps provide a wall of protection around the horse's sole and frog. This is turn acts as a cushion to protect the coffin bone.

Each time the foot is put down, a jarring vibration is sent through the hoof to the delicate leg bones. The simple act of removing too much of the frog and sole can take away those crucial cushions and lame the horse.

As Dan Brown says, "Taking off too much of the sole would be like a person putting on tissue paper shoes and running over rocks. It affects the horse even more so because it carries so much weight on its feet."

The old saying "No hoof, no horse" still rings true. If you stop to think that a horse must carry hundreds of pounds balanced on

A WILD HORSE'S HOOVES HAVE AN ABUNDANT SOLE.

four small feet, you'll realize that even the smallest injury or mistake in trimming or shoeing can cause extreme pain or other problems.

A fad in the last few years has been to trim hooves down to a small, "pretty" size. This may be pleasing to the human eye, but it's totally unnatural for the horse. A horse moves best with the feet it was born with. This is not to say that a competent farrier may not want to make corrective changes for a problem, but rather that it should be for the good of the horse, not for cosmetic reasons.

Dan Brown further states, "The important thing is to get a good horseshoer who can put on a level shoe at the proper angle. If the shoe's not level or the angle is wrong, it's like going around with one shoe higher than the other. Then the horse will be off balance and that will set in motion a lot of other problems. A horseshoer can cripple a horse or even ruin it for life, so choose someone with a good reputation."

Here are some things to consider when choosing a farrier:

- How long has the farrier been working with horses? Most farriers have had formal training or, better yet, have been apprenticed to an experienced farrier.
- How many horses does the farrier do each day? When you consider the time to come to where your horse is, gasoline, upkeep of equipment, actual working time and other factors, the price your farrier charges can amount to a poor income unless he or she does a large number of horses every day. Sometimes in an effort to stay ahead, farriers book so many horses that they are pushed to rush through jobs. It may be better to choose a farrier who charges a little more but does fewer horses.
- Ask for references.
- When your farrier is working with your horse, how does the horse behave? Does the farrier give your horse confidence? If the horse is acting up, does the farrier handle him in a firm but kind manner? Does the farrier spend a few minutes getting to know your horse? Is the farrier willing to explain what he or she is doing and why? Does the farrier work with the horse or try to overpower him?
- Remember that your horse's hooves have probably gotten long. Your farrier may want to take only a little bit off the first time and come back in a few weeks, taking several trims to return the proper angle to the hoof.

- Be sure to inform the farrier when you make the first appointment that this will be the first time the horse has ever had his feet done.
- Call at least two weeks in advance. And be polite! A good farrier is extremely important for you and your horse's happiness and future travels together.

Most wild horses seem to have strong, resilient hooves. Most of these horses have struggled to survive in rocky, mountainous areas, and nature has compensated by giving them tough hooves.

Loretta Pambianchi comments about her wild horse Ranger Bae, "His feet are like solid rocks. My blacksmith complains whenever he has to take a shoe off, because his feet are so hard." Susan Smith-

DOMESTIC HORSE HOOF. MOST DOMESTIC HORSES HAVE THINNER-WALLED HOOVES THAN WILD HORSES.

WILD HORSE HOOF.

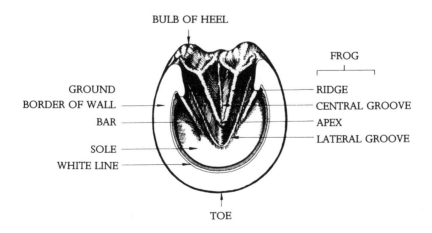

BULB OF HEEL

FROG

GROUND
BORDER OF WALL

RIDGE

BAR

CENTRAL GROOVE

APEX

LATERAL GROOVE

SOLE

WHITE LINE

TOE

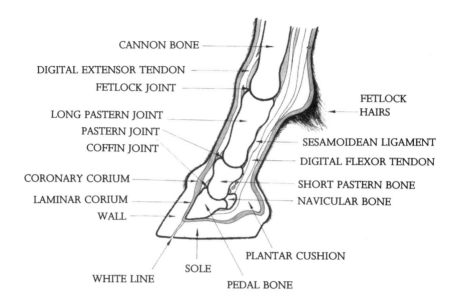

CANNON BONE

DIGITAL EXTENSOR TENDON

FETLOCK JOINT

FETLOCK
HAIRS

LONG PASTERN JOINT

PASTERN JOINT

COFFIN JOINT

SESAMOIDEAN LIGAMENT

DIGITAL FLEXOR TENDON

CORONARY CORIUM

SHORT PASTERN BONE

LAMINAR CORIUM

NAVICULAR BONE

WALL

PLANTAR CUSHION

WHITE LINE

SOLE

PEDAL BONE

PARTS OF THE FOOT AND LOWER LEG.

James, a New Jersey artist and former horseowner who rode formerly wild horses during a trail expedition in Arizona, relates, "The wild horses would run right up the rough rocky paths, with no shoes on, straight up and down, with no problems at all. They are really good practical horses."

In California, Jamie Ottinger, who competes on the "A" horse show circuit with her wild horses, remarks that her trainer is impressed with the wild horses because, "They are the only horses in the barn that never go lame."

Teaching your horse to lift his feet doesn't have to be difficult if you take your time and show the horse he has nothing to worry about. The time you spend now doing the job right will save you a lifetime of misery later.

12.

A NEW FREEDOM

Horses are happiest when they have companions to play and mingle with, in an area where they have room to run and stretch their legs.

For a wild horse that is used to roaming free, confinement in a small corral is like being locked in a closet. The corral is definitely necessary in the beginning, but now that the horse is leading well, standing still and will come when you call, it is time to move on.

The first thing to do is make a careful inspection of the pasture or paddock. Pick up soda cans, beer bottles, plastic and paper bags, old boards, wire and any other trash that's lying about.

Next check all the fencing to make sure it's in good, solid shape. Fencing is often neglected and left to fall into ruin, even in the best of stables. Electric wire fencing and, especially, barbwire are dangerous to use with any horse, but the results could be fatal with a newly gentled wild horse. An electric wire fence would be acceptable only if a board fence is behind it, and barbwire should not be used under any circumstances.

INTRODUCING THE HORSE TO THE PASTURE

After the pasture inspection, you can introduce your horse to his new space. When the field is empty, lead the horse around the whole pasture. Walk along all the boundaries so the horse knows where they are. This will be especially important if other horses will share the pasture and your horse is chased by another horse. Show the horse the water trough and feed areas.

While you are doing this, anytime the horse is startled or wants to look or sniff at something, let him have a chance to do that. This is all new, and your horse will probably be excited.

Talk to the horse in a reassuring voice. If you are impatient, the horse will get more upset and your body language will convince him that something is wrong. If you feel you are losing control of the horse, simply turn him until his attention is back on you.

As you are walking along, don't let the horse keep putting his head down to eat grass, because that could lead to the bad habit of yanking down every time he feels like eating. After you have made a tour of the field and the horse is behaving calmly, you can then let him graze while you hold the lead rope. If there is no

LEAD THE HORSE AROUND THE PASTURE OR CORRAL SO IT CAN BECOME FA-MILIAR WITH ITS NEW BOUNDARIES.

GIVE THE HORSE TIME TO LOOK AT NEW THINGS. IF IT GETS STARTLED, RE-ASSURE IT.

grass, just stand there and scratch the horse's neck or favorite itchy spot for a moment.

After a few minutes, unhook the lead, then walk away. The horse may not be aware that he's free and will follow you. That's okay—don't shoo him away. He will get the idea in a moment.

You are aiming for a very calm attitude, so the horse doesn't learn to wheel and gallop off the second the lead is unhooked. You want to teach the horse patience and good manners, while avoiding the formation of bad habits.

It is a dangerous practice to leave the horse's halter on in the pasture. A horse often uses his back foot to scratch his head and ear area, or rubs his head along a fence post. Either of these could result in the halter becoming caught, and cause serious injury or even death.

Catching your horse after he is turned out to pasture is a genuine concern. Every horseowner must weigh the risks of whether to leave the halter on or not. Specially designed breakaway halters are available for this purpose. It's a good idea to leave this type of halter on your horse until you are confident he will allow himself to be caught.

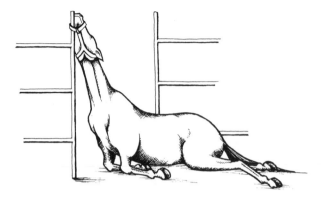

NOT CHECKING YOUR CORRAL FOR PLACES WHERE THE HALTER CAN CATCH COULD RESULT IN INJURY OR DEATH.

Let the horse check out the pasture for an hour or so alone before you bring in any more horses. The best arrangement is to put your horse in a paddock next to the field the main group of horses is in, so the horses can first meet over a fence.

A strange horse is alarming to the herd. It is a threat to their pecking order, a possible challenge to the lead horse and added competition for food and water. Even if there's only one other horse in the pasture, the two will need to work out who's the boss. Sometimes this is just a matter of a few squeals and some racing around the pasture; sometimes it comes to bites and swift kicks. In either event, disputes are usually resolved within a few hours and should not be of serious concern. The newcomer will need to earn his place in the herd, and flying hooves, bites and ears pinned back are all a part of that process.

If possible, introduce your horse to other horses on a one-on-one basis. First put out the quietest horse with the newcomer, and let them get acquainted for about an hour. Then turn out another horse, letting them get used to each other for a while. If your horse seems to be getting along okay, add another.

If there is a real bully in the herd, turn that one out in another field for a day or two. By that time, your horse will not be so overwhelmed by all the strangers and will be better able to defend himself.

It is best to keep an eye on the horses for the first week or so until the pecking order is established and things have calmed down. If after a week your horse has not been accepted or is in danger of being injured, consider moving him to another pasture or rotating the time that different horses are put out with him.

Normally the horses will settle in rather quickly. The wild horse comes from a herd-oriented environment, and natural selection has produced animals that adjust to the pecking order and direction from the lead mare or stallion. They have been taught by the herd how to interact in a group situation.

A sudden influx of green grass, especially during springtime when the grass is growing rapidly, can be harmful to the horse's digestive system. Your horse could quickly develop medical problems such as diarrhea, colic and laminitis, or founder.

If you have green grass, let the horse out for only about thirty minutes the first few days, working up to four hours a day over the next two weeks. After that, you should be able to leave the horse out all day without worry. As with any diet question, it is best to discuss this issue with your veterinarian first.

As AN ACT OF FRIENDSHIP AND SOCIAL STATUS, HORSES GROOM EACH OTHER.

RECAPTURING THE HORSE

Once the horse is out, how are you going to catch him again?

When a horse is loose in a field, the approach of a human can cause alarm. It triggers the immediate impulse "Run away!" Don't be insulted if your horse dashes off when he first sees you in the pasture.

A few weeks of gentling and good relations with people still isn't enough experience to overcome a horse's ingrained survival pattern. Horses possess a remarkable awareness of their surroundings, and they notice any change at once.

Horses' eyes are designed to pick up far-off movements, and their ears are extremely sensitive to distant sounds. All their lives they have relied on their instincts, and now your job is to get them to think rather than react blindly.

When horses are brought into a domestic setting, they need time to alter their instincts and adapt to a different kind of life. Wild horses are prized for their ability to adjust to different situations, yet it doesn't happen overnight.

Once you arrive at the point where the horse enjoys your company and the good things you bring him, like food, he will alter his survival pattern of running from people and come up to you in the field for food and companionship.

Loretta McCartney, who has worked with horses at breeding farms and show stables for more than twenty years, describes a few successful methods she uses to catch horses in the field: "Patience, bribery and jealousy are the big factors. As a prey species, horses get nervous when the predator is approaching and paying attention to them. Eye contact is threatening, so try not to look right at the horse. Also, don't walk directly to the horse you want. Pretend you are going to catch a different horse, or investigate something on the fence or ground near the horse. Then the horse will get curious: 'What's that person doing?' or 'What is that horse getting that I'm not getting?'

"If you start feeding the other horse and paying attention to it, the horse you are after will get jealous and want to come and see what's going on. When it comes up, let it eat, too. Then it is an easy matter to clip on the lead." Or if the horse is not wearing a halter, slip a rope over the neck and then slide the halter on.

If jealousy doesn't work, you can try the stop-and-go game again. Come up a little way, wait a few minutes to let the horse relax, go a little farther, stop and repeat until you reach the horse.

Another idea is to catch a quiet horse and lead him to the gate. The horse you want may follow along until he gets close enough to get caught, too. Stay alert, because at feeding time the gate can be a lively place. Hungry horses may bite and kick at each other, trying to be the first to come in.

Some owners of large numbers of horses teach their horses to exit only as their name is called. It can take several weeks to teach the horses to accept this, but in the long run this practice may prevent a "wreck" at the gate.

As Loretta McCartney says, "I view catching horses as a game, and go in there like I have all the time in the world, even if I only have five minutes. If you are in a hurry, they sense it right away by reading your body language. With a time limitation, you will be more aggressive and threatening, and that frightens them, making them more elusive. Also, habit is strong in them. Use it to your advantage and work up a routine that you always bring them in at approximately the same time every day. Giving them a treat or reward each time you catch them teaches them that they will get something good when they come up to you. Use such treats as carrot slices, apples, sugar or some grain. The trouble is that when other horses see the treats they may also be enticed. Be prepared.

A disadvantage of teaching your horse to come for a treat is that if you don't have it the horse has no reason to come to you. You may find yourself with an unhappy horse that nips at you when he completes his part of the bargain but receives no treat. As a reward, a scratch in a favorite place or a special hug may be a better choice.

Likewise, although you will be using artificial aids such as ropes when you are training your horse, it is also a good idea to teach your horse to work with you without these aids whenever possible. You always have your body and voice commands; you may not always have the aids. You and your horse must learn to work together in a true partnership.

Your horse may be an angel about being caught, or it could

sprout devilish horns. Lyn Kamer makes these suggestions for working with slippery horses: "As for catching horses that don't wish to be caught, I've tried all of the following with varying degrees of success. Any methods that worked usually only worked once; then the horse caught on and didn't fall for it again.

"1) Leave the horse out without any feed or hay. Don't put dinner out if you can't catch the horse, but do provide water. Most horses will knuckle under to this after a day or so.

"2) Remove all other horses from the area. When there's no one else to hide behind or stir up, you can usually walk a horse down in five or ten minutes.

"3) Use hay or feed to lure the horse into a smaller area, then proceed as in number two above. This was one that usually only worked once.

"4) Attach a long (20 feet or more) dragline. But getting hold of the line doesn't necessarily mean you have the horse. It can take off and either drag you or not, depending on how it feels." If you do leave a dragline on the horse, it is important that you are nearby and that there is absolutely nothing the horse can catch the rope on.

Finally, Kamer says, "My best recommendation is making sure you have a good, solid bond with the horse before you give it too much freedom. A 40-foot by 60-foot paddock is a lot of area to cover if only one person is trying to catch a horse, but it's better than a 3-acre pasture. Adding extra people can help. You really have to have persistence and patience."

Here's a trick one of the authors used to get horses into nighttime corrals from the LIFE Equine Center's 250 acres: over a two week period she began to feed the horses earlier each day until they were being fed about two hours before dark. Then she rang an old-fashioned dinner bell as loud as she could until she could see that some of the horses were watching her (anything that makes a loud noise, such as two trash-can lids, would work). Then she began making a big deal out of putting the hay out. Some of the horses saw her and came in, and then others saw those horses until the majority of the horses came in by themselves.

After about a half hour she closed the gates. Pretty soon the horses that were not paying attention started getting hungry and looked around for the other horses. Soon they were down at the corral gate wanting to get in. After they were real worried that they weren't going to get any food, she let them in. All the horses were in by dark. The next day she did the same thing. This time only a few horses were late. By the third day all the horses were in at the sound of the bell! Later she began calling each horse by name at different parts of the day. When the horse came in she would give it a special scratch or, on rare occasions, a treat. Now she can call any of the horses by name and they come. If she needs the whole gang, she just rings the bell.

IF YOUR HORSE ESCAPES

In catching your horse, your objective will be to teach the horse to come to you willingly. Remember:

- Never run after your horse; such action triggers his impulse to run away.
- Never raise your voice; the sound of your anger will only frighten him more, convincing him you are not safe to be around.
- Never get excited or be in a hurry; the horse will only become upset and run farther away.
- Think before you act; the minute or two you spend thinking a situation out can prevent a bad situation from becoming worse.

Catching your horse is something that you will be probably have to do every day for as long as you have the horse. Therefore, it is well worth the effort in the beginning to prepare your horse properly before you put him out in a large area. Make your pasture secure, and take the time to insure that coming to your call or being caught is a pleasant experience for your horse.

If your horse gets loose outside of the pasture, don't chase him. Stop a minute and think. What will make the horse *want* to return to the pasture? Unless the horse is in danger of being hit by a car, let him run around for a minute. After he gets rid of the initial excitement of being free, he will stop and look around. The area outside the horse's normal corral or pasture is strange to him, and, given the choice, he usually will return to "home" territory willingly. At this point, grab a armful of hay and calmly open the nearest corral or pasture and make a big deal of scattering the hay around. Then just walk away. If the horse is remaining calm but hasn't started walking toward the corral within a few minutes, circle *way* behind him and begin slowly walking closer until the horse calmly moves forward. If you have other people to help, they can work on either side. It is very important not to crowd the horse.

Rattling a grain bucket may persuade the horse to come back. Leading another horse past the escapee toward the corral or pasture may help. Clearing any other horses out of the pasture, then leaving the gate open with hay inside may help. Robin Rivello's mare Reno was lured back once by the rattle of a candy wrapper!

If a horse gets loose near a highway or in town, you need to assess the situation calmly and quickly. It may require an immediate call to the local police and animal control agency to block off roads. It is important to remember that the horse will run only as long as it is panicked. At this point your only recourse may be to block off areas you do not want him to go to. Instead of chasing the horse, let him run until he is tired and thus more willing to look to you for direction. Spend time talking to the horse, and approach him just as you did in the beginning, using the advance-and-retreat method. Slowly approach the horse until you can attach a lead line. If the horse starts to panic after you have the lead line on, remember to turn him in a circle until you have regained control of the situation. You will need to make a decision now whether you should walk the horse home or attempt to load him in a trailer. This will be an "on site" decision, so try to use your common sense. Do not return the horse to a pasture situation until you have more control either through bonding or training.

An escape can fast turn into a situation that could mean terrible injury or death, not only to your horse but to passengers in vehicles or other innocent parties. When you are unloading your horse for the first time, moving it to pasture or allowing the horse freedom for the first time, plan ahead. Stop and think of things that might happen and take necessary precautions.

COPING WITH PROBLEMS

If your horse continues to be hard to catch, put him back into a small corral and work on the lesson of coming when you call. Make sure you really praise and reward the horse when he comes.

Once the horse is responding to your call and you are letting him out to pasture again, occasionally catch the horse, pet him, then let him go. Another time, you can catch the horse and groom him, scratching his favorite spots for a while before releasing him. Make it a pleasure for the horse to come to you, to set up a good association with coming to you willingly.

In the event your horse has lost his halter in the pasture, don't despair. Simply approach the horse, spend time scratching him or talking and slip the lead line over the neck. Walk the horse a few steps forward so he knows you have control, then put on the halter.

While your horse is in the pasture, it is a good idea to practice moving the horse with the lead line around his neck and without the halter. Practice this lesson until the horse can be walked as smoothly with a rope around the neck as with the halter.

Your horse will have to learn "gate manners." The worst problem is the tendency of some horses to rush through the gate. Most horses find enclosed spaces uncomfortable and will need to learn to judge distances from one gate post to another. The horse will be reacting out of fear, not stubbornness, so you will need to be patient.

Remember to walk to the side of the horse so that if he bolts forward, you will not be thrown off balance or knocked down. When working around a gate for the first time, remember to use the least aggressive method first. Walk the horse around the corral; by now this should be a relaxed exercise with no resistance. Then just walk through the gate with a no-big-deal attitude. You may find that the horse offers no resistance.

If the horse resists by stopping or backing up, then turn him away from the gate. Spend a little more time just walking around before approaching the gate again. This time, stop just short of the gate, talking to the horse and reassuring him. Move the horse away from the gate. When you approach the gate, an assistant should walk behind the horse, confirming your "Walk" command while moving forward.

After the horse has gone through several times, you can reinforce the feeling that the gate is not something to fear by stopping within the gate and reassuring the horse.

If the horse still refuses to move through, you are simply going to have to outsmart him. (Remember, too many failures in one lesson can develop into a bad habit.) Try feeding your horse on just the other side of the gate. Or try backing the horse through the gate. Let him get used to the area step by step, and reward each quiet moment. Teaching the horse to go through the gate and not to rush involves going back to the basics—the lessons of standing still and walking quietly while following your commands or cues.

If the horse crowds you when he is walking, it is generally also from fear and nervousness. The horse must learn to respect your space. When he is crowding you because of fear, reassure the horse, then firmly move him over by placing your hand on his shoulder. If the horse continues to crowd you, give a firm command, "Step," while placing an elbow by his shoulder. You could also use the rounded end of a riding crop for this. Practice this exercise in an open corral. Rarely does it take more than two or three times for the horse to understand clearly that he should maintain a safe distance from you when walking.

13.

ADJUSTING TO DOMESTIC LIFE

Many things that make up our daily lives are completely alien to a wild horse. Lyn Kamer recalled that when her wild horse Twinkles first saw a dog, "Twinks started talking to the dog in little whinnies. The dog came closer and POW!, she kicked it. Then she gave the little whinnies again as if to say, 'I told you not to come any closer.'"

How your horse reacts to a dog will depend largely on the dog's signals. At the LIFE Equine Center, as many as seventy-eight wild horses right off the range have been brought in at one time. While most of the ranch dogs could walk through the corrals immediately without any problem, as soon as B.J., a Queensland Heeler who was trained to herd horses, entered the corral, the horses panicked. B.J.'s body language was "focused" on the horses, while the other dogs signaled with their body language that they were not interested in the horses.

Some horses that panic when they see a dog will run away, but others will attack, so it's important to have control over your dog when you introduce him to your horse. Burros are well known for their intense dislike of dogs, and extra care should be taken with them.

WHY HORSES GET SCARED

The way the horse's body functions helps explain why certain things frighten him. A horse cannot make rapid changes of focus with his eyes; he focuses his sight mainly by moving his head.

Horses are all nearsighted. They can see several hundred yards ahead with careful adjustment of the head, but they cannot identify an object that's farther away. They can see in three directions—forward, lateral (sideways) and behind them—but they cannot see in two ways at the same time.

Most horses have some degree of hind sight, even when the head and neck are in a straight line with the body. A streamlined horse will be able to see objects behind his own body better than a horse with a thick neck, wide shoulders or heavy hindquarters.

Horses that have wide heads and eyes placed well on the sides of their heads will see better to the side, while narrow-headed horses see better to the front. This is one reason why horses act differently from one another.

A horse's keen hearing is enhanced by ground vibrations picked up by the hooves and transmitted through the limbs. The sound is carried to the skull and registered in the internal and middle ear. Large air cavities in the skull act as sound boxes that amplify the ground vibrations. While a horse can tell that an object is coming from a long way off, he cannot identify it visually until it is quite close.

Horses seem to have an ingrained fear of things coming down on them from above. This is perhaps an inbred survival instinct left over from the time when mountain lions used to attack them by dropping on them from above. Yet it may also relate to their unique vision. Many people find that horses are uneasy with objects above their heads. Hand feeding the horse while sitting high on a fence is way to help work through this.

On the ground, everyday objects can be frightening to a wild horse. One adopter said his horse became frantic when he saw a hose in the grass, while another said that a moving electrical cord was cause for alarm.

In trying to make sense of his new world, the wild horse is relying on the way the herd reacted to danger and on his own

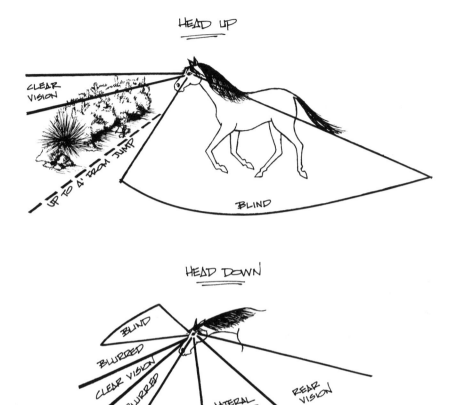

A HORSE'S VISION.

survival patterns. During the first few months after adoption, the wild horse probably goes through the kind of culture shock a cave man would experience in New York City!

GETTING USED TO DOMESTIC LIFE

Domestic life must seem very threatening to a wild horse. Besides strange animals, including people, the horse needs to learn about speeding cars, roaring machines, ear-shaking noises, flapping blankets, heavy saddles on a tender back, endless straps and lines and countless other things.

But learn he must. Teaching a horse to handle his fears and meet new things, rather than dash away, is a crucial part of his training. Since horses are designed to instantly notice the slightest changes in their surroundings, anything different startles them.

Lyn Kamer said, "They view new things with a mixture of horror and curiosity. The first time I took my winter coat off, Twinks was astounded."

Events or objects that are threatening to horses, such as paper cups or cats, may seem ridiculous to us. Yet we have to take their fears seriously because if they panic, someone could get hurt.

Many of our difficulties with horses stem from differences between how humans and horses view the world, based on the differences in our senses of sight, smell and hearing. Granted, humans have larger brains than horses, but that doesn't mean we always use them. We react from emotion and past experiences a surprising percentage of the time, without stopping to think and reason. So we can't blame wild horses for seeing a dog and giving it a kick to the moon.

Listen to what your horse is telling you. If he's afraid of something, spend extra time on the problem. To introduce your horse to potentially frightening objects, you can try doing things like:

- Leaving a hose on the ground in the corral and around the feed trough.
- Placing old, torn-up blankets around the corral.
- Hanging short pieces of rope on the fence.
- Laying a piece of plywood in front of the feed trough so the horse must step on it in order to eat.
- Putting a couple dozen aluminum cans in the trough (no sharp edges) or putting the cans in a bag tied to the fence.

Don't introduce these things all at once though; one or two at a time is enough. Give the horse time to get used to the objects in his own way.

Robin Rivello taught her mare Reno to step on things by placing open bedding bags in the stall, in front of her feed bucket. Reno had to step on them in order to eat. She spent five minutes stretching her neck like a rubber band to try and reach her food before she finally gave up and gingerly stepped on them. The next night when Robin put down a feed bag in front of the bucket, Reno promptly picked it up in her teeth and nonchalantly tossed it aside!

At the LIFE Equine Center, a common sight is a horse running around the corral with a blanket in his mouth, chasing the other horses, or two or three horses playing tug-of-war with a blanket.

As part of the horse's early training, lessons are needed in exposure to events and objects it may encounter in the world at large. The young show horse may find it very unsettling to face a crowd of noisy people at a horse show, the blaring and crackling of the loudspeaker, the smells of hot dogs and strange horses. Trail riding is fraught with modern dangers—motor bikes roaring up from behind, old furniture dumped along the path, soda cans shining in the sun, people on bicycles, stray dogs, the list is endless.

OVERCOMING FEARS

Following a reasonable program of police-horse training would be a wise course of action for the safety of you and your horse. Police-horse recruits become accustomed to various sights and sounds so they won't be frightened when they encounter them while on the job.

Again, because new lessons are stressful, a couple of things introduced in one day are enough; otherwise the horse might be overwhelmed. It's a great help if an older, experienced horse can work with the new one, settling the novice and providing a good example.

Police horses start their lessons in an enclosed area like a paddock or corral. They are gradually exposed to various objects and situations like:

• Flapping blankets, waving sheets of plastic, balloons
• Opening umbrellas, clapping hands
• Sponge balls throw at the horses, hands held over a person's head, voices through loudspeakers

- People sitting in chairs, a lot of people standing around the horse and touching him
- Hoses, tires and branches on the ground, water and mud puddles
- Rolling garbage cans, trash cans, traffic cones
- Tractors that pass by, cars that are standing still with the motor running

Take your time, be creative and use common sense about how much your horse can handle at one time. Remember, you are not threatening your horse with these things, but educating him that they are nothing to be afraid of.

Most important of all, you will teach your horse to look to you for comfort and cues about how to deal with a frightening situation. When your horse is scared, give him signals with your body and voice that everything is okay. The feeling of calm you project helps the horse keep control of his emotions.

Every lesson should be set up to insure success. Before you start, think carefully: how will my horse react to this, and what can I do to assure that he will react the way I want? Make the right action easy and the wrong action hard.

As an example from the police-horse exercises, you could put a trash can in the corral one day; the next day, put out several more. Walk your horse around the upright cans. When the horse is comfortable with that, tip one over and walk through again.

Turn the horse loose and calmly roll a trash can around the corral; when the horse accepts that, roll it in the horse's direction. If the horse becomes nervous, stop and reassure him, then begin again. Break your lessons down into small successes; only when the horse has accepted one part should you go on to the next.

While some horses can handle things quickly, others need a lot of convincing. Learn when to push and when to take a break. Make each lesson a pleasant time, so your horse will look forward to learning something new to break up the boredom of standing in the corral or pasture day after day.

Reward your horse when he has remained calm around a frightening object or situation. But remain watchful. If your horse stops and plants his feet, snorts loudly, throws his head or starts backing up, he may be on the verge of turning tail and making a run for it.

If your horse starts backing away from something scary, turn him in a circle as you did when you were teaching him to lead. Continue in the circle until the horse has calmed down. Bring the horse's attention back to you, and reassure him that he won't get eaten alive.

Once the horse is settled, move a few steps toward the object, then lead the horse away. Next bring the horse closer again, perhaps from a different angle. After a few steps, stop and praise the horse and allow him to relax. Physical contact steadies a fearful member of the herd, so stroke the horse in a soothing way. The vibrations of a low voice can have a calming effect as well.

When you come close to the object again, let the horse sniff and touch it with his nose, as horses gather information about strange things in this way. During the next few days, take the horse back to the scary thing again, even moving the object to a new setting. You want to firmly set in the horse's mind that this is a harmless object.

Teaching your horse not to be afraid of unfamiliar things and to have confidence in you will take many weeks. Continue to work with your horse until he consistently responds to your cues when he is frightened. It may take months, but this groundwork will help to develop the relationship with your horse that will make later training easier. The extra time you spend now will save time, and possibly grief, later.

INTRODUCING RIDING EQUIPMENT

Now you can start introducing your horse to such riding equipment as the saddle, bridle, pads and blankets. When you are working with your horse in the corral, hang different pieces of equipment on the fencing and allow the horse to sniff them. However, don't leave the horse alone with the equipment or the horse may nibble or chew on it for dessert.

Another suggestion is to let the horse eat some grain on the saddle pad. When he's finished munching, slowly run the saddle

To begin, rub the blanket gently all over your horse's body.

Most horse's don't like the dangling blanket straps.

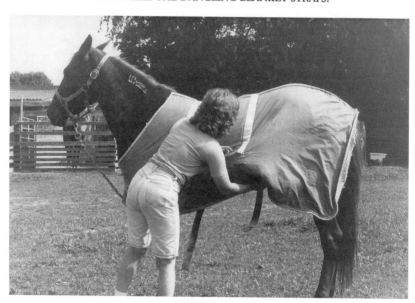

pad over the horse, starting from the neck and shoulder and proceeding onto the back. Carefully touch the horse's legs with it, too, watching to see if the horse threatens to kick.

It is a mistake to punish a horse when he is frightened, but it is also a mistake to ignore when he is deliberately acting up. Learn to recognize the difference. Some things such as biting or kicking are not acceptable under any circumstances, and this must be made clear to the horse. A swift, firm slap to the barrel or shoulder quickly communicates that kicking will not be tolerated.

When you run the saddle pad down by the horse's leg and he raises the leg, continue to hold the pad there until the horse puts down the leg. If you immediately pull away, the horse may think it can get you to stop by raising his leg.

Wild horses have never had a blanket on, so go slowly when introducing it. Many horses don't like the blanket's straps dangling down and hitting against their legs. Calm and reassure the horse with each step.

Prior to putting the blanket on, show it to the horse for a sniff and a touch, then gently touch the horse's shoulders and withers with it. Next lay it on the horse's back. As the horse accepts the blanket, calmly spread it out. Wait until the horse relaxes, then bring the straps carefully under the horse and buckle them.

All this groundwork is leading toward that wonderful day when you will have a "bombproof" horse, safe and unflappable.

14.

LOOKING AHEAD: FURTHER TRAINING AND GROUNDWORK

You look longingly at your dusty saddle and wonder, "Will my horse ever be ready to ride?" Of course, but when depends on how old or mature your hay-eating partner is. However, all the time you have spent on groundwork will make saddle training faster and easier.

Most responsible trainers agree that it is best to wait until the horse is three years old before he carries weight on his back. When you mount the horse, you will be sitting on his spinal column, the sensitive bundle of bones and nerves that sends vital messages throughout the body.

The back is a tender area for horses (and for everyone) and must be treated with care. Many problems arising in later mounted work stem not from stubbornness, but from pain or sore muscles in the back.

The trainers at the Spanish Riding School in Vienna, Austria, considered to be among the world's finest horsemen, wait until the Lipizzaners are in their fourth year before beginning their education. Horses everywhere would benefit by their example. Once a horse's legs are injured by premature or excessive work, recovery can be a slow, uphill and sometimes impossible journey.

If you are preparing the horse to be driven in harness, a well-developed two-year-old is usually ready for gradual light work, if the combined weight of the cart and driver is not too great. It is wise to have a veterinarian check the horse's legs, knees, back and general condition before starting work in harness. The veterinarian's counsel should also be sought in determining when a horse is ready to bear the weight of a rider.

PREPARATORY EDUCATION

As you wait for your horse to mature, the following matters need to be addressed for your horse's education.

• Standing quietly
• The clippers
• Vet procedures
• Loading in a trailer
• Longeing

Standing Quietly

Standing quietly seems very basic, but it's extremely important. Your horse will need to stand patiently on many occasions, such as grooming, putting on saddles and bridles, at horse shows, for the vet and farrier. Even though the horse is designed to move freely all day, he needs to learn to stand still longer than he might like. Make this a pleasant time for the horse. Stroke softly, give treats. Convince the horse it's worthwhile to stand about.

The Clippers

Horses usually object to the buzzing noise and vibration of the clippers. Since they have such sharp hearing, the noise is probably as annoying as a mosquito in a human ear.

Many people clip the winter hair from their horses so they won't become overheated when doing fast work in the spring, fall or winter. Even if you never plan to clip your horse, it's still a good idea to accustom the horse to the sound. This would be useful if the horse were to be hurt and require stitches. The vet may use clippers to remove hair in the wounded area. If you don't have horse clippers, you can use an electric shaver just to let the horse hear the buzzing sound.

Vet Procedures

During everyday handling, incorporate several actions that the vet will someday perform with your horse.

After the horse is gentle and trustworthy, get it used to letting you put your hands around his lips, teeth and gums. Be sure the horse is in a relaxed mood before you try this! During an examination, the vet will handle the lips to take a look in the mouth. The vet may need to "float," or file down, the horse's teeth or even remove some.

HOLD A HAND OVER THE EYE BRIEFLY, LIKE A VET SOMETIMES DOES TO CALM THE HORSE.

LEAD THE HORSE TO THE TRAILER AND LET IT STOP AND SNIFF.

The nostrils will also be handled by the vet during tube worming. For this procedure a small tube is inserted into the horse's nostril. The tube goes down to the stomach to administer worm medicine.

To help your vet visits go smoothly, the main thing to practice is making sure your horse is agreeable to being touched all over his body. You could also get the horse used to having your hand over his eye briefly. Vets sometimes do this to calm down an excitable horse.

Loading in a Trailer

All wild horses have ridden in trailers going to and from the adoption centers. But there the horse was sent down the loading chute directly into the trailer, so he hasn't yet learned to willingly get on one.

We strongly suggest that the first time you load your horse you have an experienced horse person on hand. Loading the horse into a trailer can quickly result in an accident in the flash of an eye, with injury to the horse and/or the handlers.

The closed-in space of the trailer may be frightening to the horse, for, unlike cats, horses don't like the dark. Generally a horse will accept a stock trailer more readily than a single or two-horse trailer.

If you own a trailer or can borrow one, an easy way to introduce your horse to the trailer is by putting it in the corral or leaving it backed up to an open gate. Check the trailer for any latches, bolts or other objects that could hurt the horse. Make sure the trailer is jacked up level and will not tilt when the horse steps in. A couple of rocks or heavy boards should be placed behind and in front of the tires to help secure the trailer.

Place the horse's morning and evening feedings inside the trailer. At first you may have to place the feed on the very edge. With each feeding, place the food farther into the trailer, until the horse is stepping in and eating out of the manger.

Feed the horse on the left side of the trailer; if you are hauling a single horse, this is the side he will be loaded on. If you are hauling two horses, the heaviest horse should go on the left side.

Once your horse is happy with eating in the trailer, you can practice actual loading. It often helps to have another horse that loads like a charm, to watch and learn from. But use a peaceful horse, one that won't kick at your horse in the trailer.

Stand by with your horse while the experienced horse is loaded onto the right side of the trailer. Bring your horse to about 3 feet away and let it look over the entrance. Say "Walk," asking your horse to go forward into the trailer.

If the horse hesitates, give him a light tap on the rump with a buggy or longe whip. Usually the horse will stop to check out the situation. Allow him to do this, then encourage it to move ahead again. If the horse starts to back up, tap him lightly with the whip.

Once the horse takes a step or two into the trailer, let him back down if he wants to. It's important to project an attitude that this is not a scary thing but simply another experience.

Keep asking the horse to step into the trailer until he gains enough confidence to go all the way in. Then reward him with a treat to show him you are well pleased. Let the horse spend a little time eating, then ask him to back out with your command "Back."

Don't let the horse rush. If he hurries he may hit his head on the ceiling or slip and fall. Speak calmly to settle the horse and have him take one slow step backward at a time.

GAINING CONFIDENCE, DELTA AGREES TO STEP UP INTO THE TRAILER.

BRING YOUR HORSE IN AND OUT SEVERAL TIMES TO HELP IT UNDERSTAND THAT TRAILERING IS NO BIG DEAL. IF THE HORSE IS SCARED OR RESISTS, SETTLE IT BEFORE PROCEEDING.

DELTA GETS A REWARD FOR STANDING QUIETLY IN THE TRAILER.

BACKING OFF THE TRAILER—STEPPING OUT INTO THE UNKNOWN—IS FRIGHTENING, SO GO SLOW AND EASY.

Load the horse another time or two, then let him finish his meal inside the trailer. If after several tries the horse still resists getting on the trailer, don't force the horse on or make a big issue of it. Find some experienced help and try again another day. Waiting is better than forcing the horse now and having to retrain him down the road. A problem loader is a real headache every time he's faced with a trailer.

Longeing

This is an exercise in which the trainer stands at the center of a ring or corral with the horse circling around. A 25-foot longe line is attached to the horse's halter, or to a cavesson, a special piece of equipment used for longeing.

Longeing is an excellent way to build up the horse's muscle tone. Most wild horses have been in captivity for a few months, standing around in holding pens eating hay, so their muscle tone needs improving. Longeing also helps exercise both sides of the body.

Start out by snapping the longe line onto the inside ring of the halter, or on the top ring of the cavesson. Lead the horse in a circle to the left, holding the longe line in your left, or inside, hand.

After a few minutes of walking around, have a helper quietly bring in a longe whip, which is a slender whip about 5 feet in length, and give it to the trainer. Stop and let the horse see and sniff the whip, then carefully stroke the horse with it, all over his body.

Now the assistant can lead the horse in a circle at a walk, while the trainer stays in the middle walking a smaller circle. Working the horse near the fencing of the ring or corral gives the horse boundaries and helps to focus his attention.

Gradually let the longe line out to about 15 feet. If the line is too long, it's easy for the horse to get distracted. As he's walking, the whip should be pointed at the middle of the horse's hind legs.

After a minute or two say "Whoa," vibrate the line slightly, switch the whip to point in front of the horse, and have the helper stop him. Praise your horse if he is cooperating. To walk on, say "Walk" and point the whip at the horse's croup (the top of his hindquarters). If he doesn't understand, give him a little tap there with the whip to help him respond.

Practice walking forward and then stopping a couple of times. Ask your helper to walk ahead as soon as you say "Walk" and to stop when you say "Whoa." This gives the horse an example to follow. To establish clear signals, use the same command and tone of voice each time.

After the horse catches on, change the direction and longe him from the right side. Clip the line on the right ring of his halter. Now the line will be in your right hand and whip in your left.

If while longeing the horse moves toward you, ask the helper to take him back to the original circle. If you're working alone, encourage the horse to stay out there by pointing the whip at the girth area and stepping toward him.

Urge him on with your voice. During this training, your voice will be giving most of the signals. Normally the whip doesn't need to touch the horse except for small taps to move him forward if he doesn't respond to voice commands. Never use the whip to hit the horse on the head. Anger can sometimes overtake us when things go wrong. The whip could injure the horse's eye and make him scared of the whip. We're using the whip to signal the horse, not for punishment.

For the first lessons, a few minutes of longeing are plenty. We just want the horse to catch onto the idea of staying out on the circle, going forward and stopping on command. Once the horse understands this, try the next lesson without the assistant.

Up to now we've been doing our work at the walk, but the trot is the best gait for building up muscles and balance. Since the trot is a two-beat gait, it exercises both sides of the body equally. For trotting, we need to give the horse more room, so play out the line to about 20 feet.

To ask for the trot, raise the whip up to the height of the horse's tail, then say "Trot." If the horse doesn't understand, you could tap the ground behind the horse with the whip, or you might want to ask your helper to trot beside the horse. Be aware that a running person may startle him, so your helper should be careful.

Once the horse is trotting along smoothly, praise him so he knows that's what you wanted. To slow him back to a walk, in a quiet voice say "Walk" *very* slowly. Vibrate the line and bring the whip around so that it's pointing in front of the horse. This should help him come back to a walk.

If at other times while trotting the horse gets excited and starts going too fast or cantering, remain calm. Vibrate the line and use a soft voice to settle him. If he keeps going faster, draw in the line with a give-and-take motion and make the circle smaller and smaller. Eventually he will have to slow down to keep his balance. Make sure you soothe the horse when he's walking again. He needs to be quiet before you continue with the lesson.

Once the horse is working regularly on the longe, use as large a circle as possible. Working in small circles can put too much strain a young horse's legs and may injure them. When the horse is going well at the walk and trot, you can introduce the canter or lope. If he learns the word for canter, it will be useful later in work under saddle.

It's easiest to teach the horse to break into a canter from the trot. When the horse is trotting, make the circle smaller. Next,

THE TROT EXERCISES BOTH SIDES OF THE BODY.

lengthen the line for a larger circle and then say "Canter." Point the whip above the hindquarters and maybe snap the lash.

When this is first attempted, some horses will just trot faster. In that case, slow the horse down with your voice and make the circle smaller, then try again. When you're successful, praise him and let him canter a few circles.

The canter is useful to give variety to the lessons, but most longe work is done at the trot. Vary the time trotting with short and then longer periods. Practice frequent transitions between the walk and trot. This keeps the horse alert and exercises important muscles. End the lessons with quiet walking and a session of praise.

The number of weeks you spend working on the longe depends on your horse's age and your training goals. For a horse five years old or older, two or three months is adequate to develop better muscle tone and balance. With younger horses, longeing can be useful to build confidence and manners, but keep the work light.

Later on in your training program, longeing can be used on days when you can't ride and your horse needs exercise.

INTRODUCING THE BIT, BRIDLE AND SADDLE

The Bit

Popular bits on which to start young horses are those in the snaffle family:

- The rubber-covered D-ring snaffle
- The O-ring or eggbutt snaffle
- The straight bar or Mullen snaffle

Bits come in different sizes, and selecting the correct size for your horse's mouth is very important. If this is your first time buying a bit, take along an experienced friend or ask the saddle shop person for help. The number of bits available is rather overwhelming.

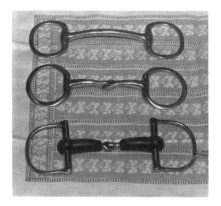

POPULAR BITS FOR STARTING HORSES. FROM TOP TO BOTTOM: THE STRAIGHT BAR, OR MULLEN SNAFFLE, THE EGGBUTT SNAFFLE AND THE RUBBER-COVERED D-RING SNAFFLE. (PHOTO COURTESY OF BOB'S SADDLE SHOP, MOUNT HOLLY, NEW JERSEY)

In general, the thicker the bit, the easier it is on the mouth. Consequently, thinner bits have a stronger action on the tongue and bars of the horse's mouth. Bits that are jointed, or "broken," in the middle, like the snaffle, relieve some pressure on the tongue. However, the snaffle can also pinch the tongue and injure the roof of the mouth if it's used in a rough, unthinking way.

In the beginning, the milder the bit you can use, the better. You can always determine later whether the horse needs another bit for balance or control. Stronger bits are sometimes helpful as you reschool an aggressive or spoiled horse, but they should never be used with young, uneducated horses.

In general, don't use the curb bits that come with many western bridles for your horse's first bit. The action is too severe for an innocent mouth.

Two types of bridles made to be used without bits are the hackamore and the bosal. They are designed to put pressure on the sensitive nose when the reins are applied. You should be experienced with a hackamore or bosal before using it on your horse because sudden pressure on the nose can cause pain.

The founder of the TT.E.A.M. Method, Linda Tellington-Jones, recommends starting young horses in a bitless bridle called a Lindell. The Lindell works directly on the horse's nose without exerting any pressure on the nerves on either side of the head. The Lindell is available through the TT.E.A.M. catalog. (TT.E.A.M. Club, Site 20, Comp. 9, RR 1, Vernon, B.C., Canada V1T 6L4. The catalog costs $3, which will be refunded with the first order.)

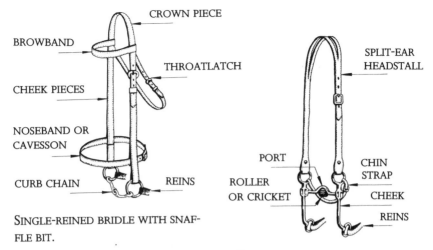

CROWN PIECE

BROWBAND

CHEEK PIECES

NOSEBAND OR
CAVESSON

THROATLATCH

CURB CHAIN

REINS

SINGLE-REINED BRIDLE WITH SNAF-
FLE BIT.

SPLIT-EAR
HEADSTALL

PORT

CHIN
STRAP

ROLLER
OR CRICKET

CHEEK

REINS

SPLIT-EARED BRIDLE WITH HALF-
BREED BIT.

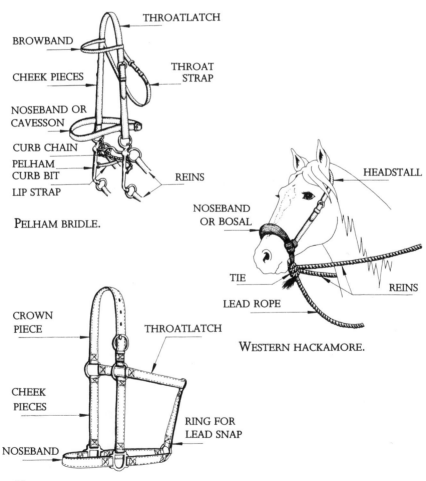

THROATLATCH

BROWBAND

CHEEK PIECES

THROAT
STRAP

NOSEBAND OR
CAVESSON

CURB CHAIN

PELHAM
CURB BIT

REINS

LIP STRAP

PELHAM BRIDLE.

HEADSTALL

NOSEBAND
OR BOSAL

TIE

REINS

LEAD ROPE

WESTERN HACKAMORE.

CROWN
PIECE

THROATLATCH

CHEEK
PIECES

RING FOR
LEAD SNAP

NOSEBAND

HALTER.

The Bridle

The horse should be allowed to get used to having a bit in his mouth before he learns what the reins are for.

The mouth is a sensitive area where something crucial to survival happens: *eating.* To facilitate the tasting and chewing of food, Mother Nature placed a lot of nerve endings in the mouth. Be considerate of the horse's mouth. To prepare your horse for having a bit in his mouth, take a few moments each time you work with him and place your thumb in the side of his mouth. Wiggle your thumb and the horse will open his mouth. (This is similar to the exercises for vet procedures.)

The corners of the horse's mouth are tender as are the gums, or bars, where the bit will lie. When you first start putting the bit in, leave it in for only a few minutes. The horse needs to develop calluses on the bars before he's asked to work in and respond to the bit.

Introducing the bridle should not present a problem because the headstall of the bridle is like the halter your horse is used to. First remove the reins and the bit, and let the horse smell the headstall. Then slip it on.

When the horse accepts this, remove the headstall and reattach the bit. Hold the bit in your hands for a few moments to warm it up. Some trainers suggest putting a little molasses or corn syrup on the bit to make it more acceptable to the horse.

Hold the bit in your left hand and the headstall in your right. Place your left thumb in the side of the mouth to get the horse to open up. When he does, guide the bit over the tongue and into the mouth. Be careful not to bang the teeth. If there is nothing sweet on it, the rubber or metal taste of the bit may cause the horse to pull back.

Try again until the horse accepts the bit hanging loosely in the mouth, but high enough to avoid hitting the teeth. Now slip the headstall on, buckle the browband and the throatlatch strap, if your bridle has one. The bit should be about an inch lower than the corner of the mouth. Leave the bit and headstall on for a few minutes. Some trainers let the horse eat hay or grain with the bridle on, but this may cause discomfort or small cuts in the mouth if hay or grain get stuck around the bit.

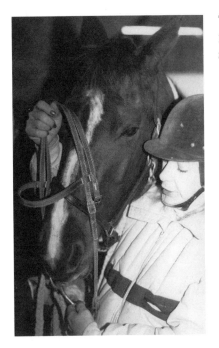

To put on the bridle hold the bit in your left hand, the headstall in your right.

Adjusting the length of the creek straps.

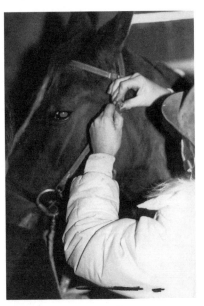

The trainer walks behind, signaling the turns.

Every day increase the length of time your horse has the bit in his mouth, bringing the bit closer to the corners of the mouth. Your horse is now ready for an introduction to the reins. One way to teach the horse to take direction from the reins is by ground driving. This consists of attaching lines approximately 25 feet long to the bridle. The trainer walks in back of the horse and signals it to turn and stop. Although some horse trainers skip this step, it is an excellent way to introduce your horse to the reins when your horse is too young to carry a rider.

If a horse is going to learn to drive, this is a necessary step. Teaching a horse to drive is a subject unto itself. Consult one of the many good books available for information.

The Saddle

Since the horse has accepted ropes around his legs and sides from previous lessons, introducing the saddle should go smoothly. When the big day comes when you plan to slide the saddle onto your horse's unsuspecting back, let the horse outside to play first.

Later, in a small corral or stall, show the horse the saddle blanket or pad. Rub it gently all over his body, being careful in ticklish spots. Once the horse pays no attention to the pad, bring the saddle over for it to sniff. Walk around the horse holding the saddle, letting it creak and jingle. Next bring over the girth or cinch, and rub that slowly on the horse's body.

Place the saddle pad well up on the withers, then slide it backward until it's in position. This insures that the hair will lie smooth under the pad. Remove the stirrups from the saddle or tie them up so they don't hit the horse as you put the saddle on.

A lightweight saddle is best for these first lessons. Let the horse smell the saddle before lifting it onto his back. It may be helpful to have an assistant at the horse's head.

Ease the saddle on the back. Don't let it drop because that may hurt or startle the horse. Stroke and praise your horse. Then practice putting the saddle on and taking it off several times.

Now take the saddle off and put on the girth. Lay the girth over the top of the saddle before you lower the saddle back on the horse. If the girth dangles, it could flap around and frighten the horse.

Let the girth down easy. When you are on the left side, reach under and bring the girth up to the billet, or tie straps. Take a few minutes to let the horse feel the girth on his stomach. When the horse is calm, attach the girth.

Don't pull the girth up so tight that it's painful for the horse, but make it secure enough so that the saddle does not slip. Walk the horse forward, paying close attention to see that the saddle is not sliding.

Continue walking the horse, then check the girth again. You may want to tighten it one or two holes. Now put the horse on the longe line, working it at the walk, trot and canter. Don't be surprised if your horse gives a few bucks to test this strange feeling.

When the horse is moving freely, stop and remove the longe line. Let the horse have free movement around the corral. Again, a little bucking is normal. If your horse starts to lie down, move quickly forward and, using sharp voice commands, get the horse up.

ATTACH THE GIRTH LOOSELY AT FIRST.

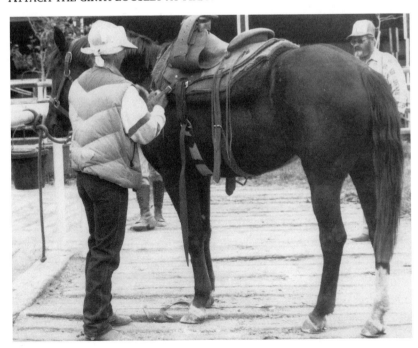

During the next few days, gradually increase the length of time the saddle is on. Some days tie the horse up, with the saddle on for a while. When the horse is relaxed with the saddle on, let the stirrups down in a normal position and repeat the exercises above.

The charts on pages 184 to 191 illustrate the different types of bridles and saddles. Well-made tack will last a lifetime if it is taken care of properly. The financial investment can be anywhere from $100.00 for a used saddle to thousands of dollars for a performance or show saddle.

Each type of riding requires different types of tack, and your own personal style or preference, plus the conformation of your horse, should all be taken into consideration when you purchase needed equipment.

Since your horse will mature and gain weight as he becomes physically fit, we do not recommend that you buy a saddle as soon as you adopt your horse. You may want to borrow a variety of saddles until you are familiar with the different styles.

Tack shops are eager to help buyers pick the correct-fitting saddle for their horse. A poor-fitting saddle can cause painful sores or even permanent damage, so it's important to have experienced help in choosing a saddle for your horse.

For introducing the rider, the methods are the same for the wild horse as for any young horse. There are many different styles and philosophies about the right way to proceed, so talk to professional horse trainers whom you respect. You could also consult books that are in accord with your style of working with horses.

Build up the work gradually, and keep it interesting and enjoyable for you and your horse. As animal consultant Penelope Smith says on her audiotape *Understanding Animal Viewpoints*, "I find that very intelligent horses—and most of them are, are best worked by showing them a new pattern and going over it a few times until they have it roughly, but not drumming it until it's stressful. . . . Make training light and fun, and your horse will do better at each practice session."

Try to be flexible about the goals you want to achieve with your horse. If you have your heart set on having a dressage horse and your horse is clearly not cut out for it, try something else. Experiment, for your horse may truly blossom at another activity.

Both you and your horse have come a long way since that first day at the adoption center. Your hard work has paid off, because

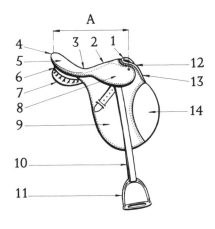

ENGLISH SADDLE

Parts of the English saddle.

A. CORRECT SEAT MEASUREMENT

1. CUTBACK
2. TWIST
3. DIP
4. CANTLE
5. SEAT
6. PANEL FACING
7. PANEL
8. SKIRT
9. FLAP
10. STIRRUP LEATHER
11. STIRRUP
12. FORE PIECE
13. PANEL FACING
14. KNEE ROLL

Parts of the Western saddle.

A. CORRECT SEAT MEASUREMENT

1. SEAT
2. CANTLE FRONT
3. CANTLE BINDER
4. BACK JOCKEY
5. SKIRT
6. REAR RIGGING DEE
7. SIDE JOCKEY OR FRONT SKIRT
8. SADDLE STRINGS
9. FLANK BILLET
10. FLANK CINCHA BODY CENTER
11. FLANK CINCHA CONNECTOR STRAP
12. HORN CAP OR HEAD
13. HORN NECK
14. FORK BINDING
15. FORK OR SWELL
16. THE STRAP HOLDER
17. FRONT JOCKEY
18. FRONT RIGGING DEE
19. THE STRAP OR SHORT LATIGO
20. FENDER
21. FRONT GIRTH
22. HOBBLE STRAP

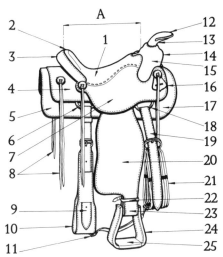

WESTERN SADDLE

23. STIRRUP LEATHER
24. STIRRUP
25. TREAD COVER

CLOVE HITCH

BOWLINE

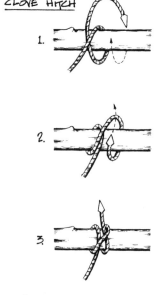

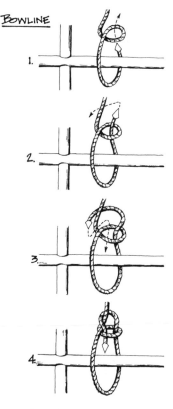

A SIMPLE CLOVE HITCH TIED AROUND THE HITCH RAIL WILL KEEP THE LEAD ROPE FROM SLIDING ALONG THE RAIL.

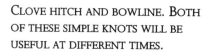

CLOVE HITCH AND BOWLINE. BOTH OF THESE SIMPLE KNOTS WILL BE USEFUL AT DIFFERENT TIMES.

THE BOWLINE IS NOT A SLIP KNOT AND WILL REMAIN EASY TO UNTIE NO MATTER HOW HARD THE HORSE PULLS BACK.

a formerly wild, frightened horse now trusts you and looks to you for guidance, and is a true friend and partner.

As adopter Loretta Pambianchi remarked, "Adopting a wild horse is a challenge, but the rewards are great. My wild horse, Ranger Bae, has really adapted to this kind of life. I trained him to the way I ride, and now I can put anybody on him. He's just fantastic and gives his all. He can really go the distance, finish up and be ready for more. I waited fifteen years for a horse like him, and it was well worth it."

If you haven't already adopted a wild horse, challenge yourself! Ride with pride as you experience the adventure of owning one of America's wild horses.

.15.

TODAY'S WORKING WILD HORSES

The ancestors of the wild horse once chased buffalo with Native Americans, carried the mountain man into the wilderness, pulled the pioneers' plows and wagons as they made a new life in the West and helped cattlemen establish vast empires.

As part of man's efforts to improve the wild herds, some of the best horse breeds were added to the noble Spanish horses of the conquistadors: horses such as the tough, versatile Morgan, the beautiful Arabian, and its cousins (unequaled for speed) the Thoroughbred and the Standardbred as well as the powerful draft breeds like the Clydesdale and the Percheron.

In today's wild horses, the various qualities of these different breeds are all rolled into one horse! This is why you'll hear horsemen such as Owen Badgett, who was raised on a Montana cattle ranch and who now works as a wrangler for the BLM, say, "The thing about wild horses is that there's one for everybody. One that you can teach to drive, one to work cattle, do dressage, go on trails, jump, anything you want."

Dan Brown and Callie Thornburgh, who own High Sierra Training in Inyokern, California, almost always have two or three wild horses they are training for clients. They also use former wild horses in riding lessons, to work cattle, for roping lessons and for wilderness trail rides into the South Sierra Mountains. Dan relates, "My grandfather always told me it was survival of the fittest out on the range, and he was right. These wild horses have survived, and they're tough."

Besides being physically strong from having to survive under harsh conditions, wild horses are also mentally healthy from being raised by the herd. The foals are with their mothers for a natural length of time, learning how to have fun, what food to eat, to depend on each other and to have respect for their elders.

Once captured and with proper care, the majority of wild horses adapt quickly to their new lives, becoming one of the most versatile and hard-working horses.

Available coast to coast through the Adopt-A-Horse program, wild horses are used for everything from endurance riding to show jumping, from cattle roping to pleasure riding. They can truly be called a "horse for all seasons and reasons!"

Wild horses and the city don't usually mix, but in the Bronx, in the New York City neighborhood called City Island, wild horses are giving city children a chance to see one up close. At the North Wind Institute, Executive Director Michael Sandlofer uses several wild horses for educational programs such as horse history and biology. Sandlofer has also trained a few draft-type wild horses, known as the Bronxdales, to pull wagons, carriages and trolleys. The horses pull the wagons for North Wind exhibits in parades, for wildlife tours, and also for the Pollution Patrol. This wagon carries volunteers who patrol the woods to collect refuse for the benefit of area residents. The Institute's address is: North Wind Institute, North Wind Museum, 610 City Island Avenue, City Island, Bronx, New York 10464.

In the sport of endurance riding, the year 1990 saw a wild horse become the National Champion Middleweight Endurance Horse. This competition consisted of a series of three rides: a 100-mile ride in Oregon, a 100-mile ride in Texas, and a 150-mile ride (over two days) in Nevada.

The human half of this hardworking team, Naomi Tyler, related, "Mustang Lady was originally from the rugged Owyhee Mountains of Idaho. I adopted her as a lame two-year-old in 1982." She was hurt during the roundup and aborted her foal.

"Mustang Lady has been competing in endurance riding for five years, and after 4,000 miles of competition, she is still going strong." Some of her accomplishments are:

1990—Tevis Cup 100-Mile Ride: placed second out of 238 horses.
1989—North American Championship 100-Mile Team: a Bronze Medal.
1989—North American Middleweight Endurance Ride Championships: placed third.
1988—Tevis Cup 100-Mile Ride: placed sixteenth out of 225 horses.

As Naomi says, "We'd like to see more wild horses on the endurance trail, because they're made for it!"

In New Jersey, adopter Lyn Kamer, who competes successfully in endurance riding up and down the East Coast, remarks, "My mare Twinkles has a lot of heart, and the rapport we have is unlike any I have ever had with a horse before. I am 100 percent sold on these horses. I just wish I had the room, time and money for more!"

Robin Rivello and her wild horse Reno won endurance-ride championships in their first year together. Rivello relates, "Wild horses are great for anyone who wants a good horse at a good price—if they can put the time and effort into it. Gentling a wild horse is very rewarding because each new thing they can do is so exciting.

NAOMI TYLER OF BOISE, IDAHO, WITH MUSTANG LADY AT A 100-MILE RIDE IN DAMMERON VALLEY, UTAH, IN 1989. IN THIS EVENT THEY PLACED SECOND OVERALL AND WON THE BEST CONDITION AWARD. (COURTESY OF COLOR-LAND PHOTO, ST. GEORGE, UTAH)

TWINKLES IS A GOOD EXAMPLE OF THE WILD HORSE'S VERSATILITY. SHE HAS WON COMPETITIVE TRAIL RIDES AND IS ALSO USED BY HER OWNER FOR PLEASURE RIDING AND DRIVING.

"If you run into problems, you have to figure out what's going to work with this horse. Have faith: it gets better. It may take longer, maybe months longer, but they will come around. After all Reno and I have been through together, I wouldn't trade her for anything!"

Iris Fitzpatrick, also an endurance rider with Tevis Cup experience and a wild horse adopter, says, "If you have experience with horses, I'd definitely recommend wild horses. They're good, solid horses."

In Barstow, California, there are even wild horses in the Marines! The Marine Corps Mounted Color Guard performs in parades and at other events, and has matched Palomino wild horses in their unit.

Also in California, wild horses are becoming noticeable at horse shows when the ribbons are handed out. Dr. Philip Ottinger says that when he watches his daughter, Jamie, compete with their wild horses, "It's very satisfying to see a horse that we adopted for $125 winning over $25,000 show horses!" Jamie adds that the things she likes best about wild horses, besides their winning performance,

TERESA FINK LEADING JASON RICH-
ARDS IN A LEAD LINE CLASS WITH
PRAIRIE STAR AT A HORSE SHOW AT
THE LEWISBERRY ADOPTION CEN-
TER. TERESA AND JASON ARE FROM
NEW YORK. (COURTESY OF BLM, EASTERN
STATES OFFICE, ALEXANDRIA, VIRGINIA)

ALTHOUGH TRUCKS ARE NOW
COMMON ON THE RANCH, MANY
MODERN-DAY COWBOYS STILL USE
HORSES TO WORK CATTLE. (COUR-
TESY OF BLM, BILLINGS, MONTANA)

is that "you can take them to a horse show, then go home and go on a trail ride or to the beach. You don't have to worry about hurting them, because they're so tough and strong."

Another success story is Teresa Fink and Prairie Star. Prairie Star was adopted by Shirley Wagner of New York in 1982. Interested in showing people how useful and good-looking wild horses can be, Ms. Wagner began training Prairie Star for the show ring. Teresa Fink, a young but skillful rider, started showing Prairie Star at local 4-H events. After a few years, Teresa and Prairie Star were winning blue ribbons at the New York State Fair. They were successful in Pony Stock Seat Equitation, Western Pleasure and Trail, and in English classes as well.

ONYX, A FORMER WILD HORSE, AND JAMIE OTTINGER, A CALIFORNIA STATE HORSEMAN'S ASSOCIATION JUNIOR JUMPER FINALIST IN 1989, COMPETE ON THE A CIRCUIT. (COURTESY PHILIP OTTINGER)

THIS FORMER WILD HORSE AND HIS RIDER ECHO THE HOOFBEATS OF YESTERDAY. (COURTESY OF BLM EASTERN STATES OFFICE, ALEXANDRIA, VIRGINIA)

Loretta Pambianchi first began training her wild horse Ranger Bae for English events but discovered that he loved the excitement of barrel racing and gymkhana classes. She remarks, "In the slow classes he was bored to death. His calling was the exciting events because he loves to run. His best qualities are his speed and agility, and doing long hours on the trail. When we began showing and he started putting ribbons on the wall, I liked that! I'd line up the blue ribbons on the stall door the night before a show and say, 'See these? We want more!' People say horses are color-blind, but I think my wild horse sees rainbows."

The following photographs spotlight former wild horses who through good nutrition, care and intelligent handling by their adopters have become shining examples of the potential of today's working wild horses.

AFTERWORD

The mountains and the lands of the West are powerfully beautiful—dignified and majestic—as are the horses that live among them.

Wild horses are born with the colors of the mountains upon them: the browns, reds and blues, the dapple and flea-speckled grays and the white of the snow-covered peaks.

They are as tough as the steep rocky hills, and when they gallop, their hoofbeats resound like distant thunder.

Horses are a nation that finds joy in living and in friendship. They play with unabashed gusto, teasing and tackling and playing catch me if you can. Sometimes they hurt each other, but forgiveness comes swiftly. Soon they are resting side by side.

The mares watch the fillies and colts playing, standing close by like schoolmarms ready to break up the mock battles if they get too rough. The words "band," "harem" and "herd" are used to describe groupings of horses, but they fail to relay the intensity of the family of young and old: fillies, colts and mares, and the stallion that guards them all. They have close bonds of friendship and stinging rivalries, but they don't harbor the human fault of holding a grudge. They are a nation unto themselves and in harmony with their environment.

The history of man and horse is woven into a story more than 5,000 years old. Horses have been at the heart of that tapestry, a vivid patchwork of conquest as man triumphed over his fellow humans and the good earth. The horse has brought us from humble caves and huts to the palaces of kings, tilled the land, carried produce to market, endured our weight going home and then freed our hearts as we raced over the mountain for the sheer joy of the wind in our hair.

Yet, in some communities, wild horses and burros have been classified as an overpopulating nuisance akin to rats in the cellar. But rats have never taken a bullet in our wars or fallen to the ground struggling to clear our lands or broken a leg racing for our entertainment.

Yes, populations of wild horses and burros need to be adjusted to the conditions where they now live, confined by fences and government regulations. Where there are too many for the land to support, they need to be removed, for the benefit of themselves and the land.

But it is not humane to let them "naturally" starve or die of thirst in the unnatural environment we have created for them. Once we remove the "excess," for whatever reason, man has the responsibility to see that they are cared for properly, as true friends and companions.

Horses need to have enough space to run freely and to live with other horses as nature intended. They can then express their true joy in being alive, so that their power and majesty can shine forth like a sunrise over the mountains.

When we began this book it seemed such a simple task. Yet we found at each step of the way a hundred questions, and most likely there are a hundred more we haven't answered. We hope our humble efforts help you.

If you find there are problems or questions we have not answered, and if you feel we can be of help, feel free to write to us in care of the LIFE Foundation, 6455 N. Quail, Inyokern, CA 93527. Please include your phone number and we will call you, collect, as soon as possible.

APPENDIX 1.
BUREAU OF LAND MANAGEMENT OFFICES FOR THE ADOPT-A-HORSE OR BURRO PROGRAM

Carr's Wild Horse Center
4420 State Route 665
London, Ohio 43140

Ridgecrest Wild Horse and Burro
Holding Facility
300 South Richman Road
Ridgecrest, California 93555

Rock Springs District Office
P. O. Box 1869
Rock Springs, Wyoming 82902

Burns BLM Wild Horse Corrals
HC 74-12533, Highway 20 West
Hines, Oregon 97738

Palomino Valley Wild Horse and
Burro Adoption Center
P. O. Box 3270
Sparks, Nevada 89432

Adopt-A-Horse
Eastern States Office
350 South Pickett Street
Alexandria, Virginia 22304
Handling the states of Virginia, Pennsylvania, Kentucky, Maryland, Connecticut, Delaware, Maine, Massachusetts, New Hampshire, New Jersey, Rhode Island, Vermont, New York and the District of Columbia

Adopt-A-Horse
Milwaukee District Office
310 West Wisconsin Avenue
Suite 225
P. O. Box 631
Milwaukee, Wisconsin 53203
Handling the states of Illinois, Minnesota, Wisconsin, Iowa, Ohio, Indiana, Michigan, Missouri, West Virginia

Adopt-A-Horse
Jackson District Office
411 Briarwood Drive #404
Jackson, Mississippi 39206
Handling the states of Alabama,
North Carolina, Florida, Georgia,
Alaska, South Carolina, Tennessee, Louisiana, Mississippi

Adopt-A-Horse
Bureau of Land Management
200 N.W. 5th, Room 548
Oklahoma City, Oklahoma 73102
Handling the states of Oklahoma,
Kansas, Texas, Minnesota

Adopt-A-Horse
Phoenix District
2015 West Deer Valley Road
Phoenix, Arizona 85027

Adopt-A-Horse
3380 Americana Terrace
Boise, Idaho 83706

Adopt-A-Horse
Utah State Office
P. O. Box 45155
324 South State Street, Suite 301
Salt Lake City, Utah 84145-0155

Adopt-A-Horse
BLM Spokane District
East 4217 Main Avenue
Spokane, Washington 99202

Adopt-A-Horse
2800 Cottage Way
Sacramento, California 95825

Adopt-A-Horse
BLM Canon City District
P. O. Box 2200
Canon City, Colorado 81215-2200

Adopt-A-Horse
Bureau of Land Management
P. O. Box 36800
Billings, Montana 59107
Handling the states of Montana,
South Dakota, North Dakota

APPENDIX 2.
SAMPLE FORMS

Wild Free-Roaming Horse or Burro

Certificate of Title

is hereby granted title to the animal described below,
in accordance with the Act of 1971, Public Law 92-195,
as amended by Public Law 95-514.

FREEZE MARK NUMBER

_____   _____

SIGNALMENT KEY   Bureau of Land Management

_____   _____
                                                                          Date
CERTIFICATE NUMBER

_____

U. S. Department of the Interior   Bureau of Land Management

Form 4710-10
(August 1989)

UNITED STATES
DEPARTMENT OF THE INTERIOR
BUREAU OF LAND MANAGEMENT

FORM APPROVED
OMB NO. 1004-0042
Expires: February 28, 1991

APPLICATION FOR ADOPTION OF WILD HORSE(S) OR BURRO(S)

APPLICANT'S LAST NAME   FIRST   M.I.

STREET ADDRESS OR P.O. BOX

CITY   STATE   ZIP CODE

DRIVER'S LICENSE NO.   STATE   BIRTHDATE

HOME PHONE *(include area code)*   BUSINESS PHONE *(include area code)*

Number of animals requested for adoption: Horses [ ][ ][ ]   Burros [ ][ ][ ]

Please answer the following questions:

1. Have you read and do you understand the PROHIBITED ACTS and the TERMS OF ADOPTION on the reverse side? ☐ Yes ☐ No

2. Describe the facilities that will be provided to the animals you have requested.

   a. Shelter size, height, and construction materials:

   b. Corral size, fence height and construction materials:

   c. Feed, water, and pasture:

   d. Transport equipment:

3. Will more than four untitled wild horses or burros be kept at the location where you will keep the animals requested in this application? ☐ Yes ☐ No

4. Will someone other than you select or care for the animals requested? ☐ Yes ☐ No

5. Have you previously adopted animals through the Federal Government's Wild Horse and Burro Adoption Program? ☐ Yes ☐ No

6. Have you ever been convicted of abuse or inhumane treatment of animals, violation of the Wild Free Roaming Horse and Burro Act or the Wild Horse and Burro Regulations? ☐ Yes ☐ No

_____   _____
(Signature of Applicant)   (Date)

Title 18 U.S.C. Section 1001, makes it a crime for any person knowingly and willfully to make to any department or agency of the United States any false, fictitious, or fraudulent statements or representation as to any matter within its jurisdiction.

FOR BLM USE ONLY

Application *(check appropriate box)* ☐ Approved ☐ Disapproved *(If "disapproved," give reason.)*

                                                   DATE   STATE

_____
(Signature of Authorized Officer)   Mo   Day   Yr

(Instructions on reverse)

INDEX

Figures in *italics* refer to illustrations.